THE
HELICOPTER
PILOT'S MANUAL

VOLUME 1

Principles of Flight and Helicopter Handling

Norman Bailey

THE CROWOOD PRESS

First published in 1996 by
Airlife Publishing, an imprint of
The Crowood Press Ltd
Ramsbury, Marlborough
Wiltshire SN8 2HR

www.crowood.com

New edition 2008

British Library Cataloguing-in-Publication Data
A catalogue record for this book is available from the British Library.

ISBN   978 1 86126 982 9

Typeset by SR Nova Pvt Ltd., Bangalore, India

Printed and bound in Singapore by Craft Print International

THE
HELICOPTER
PILOT'S MANUAL

VOLUME 1

Principles of Flight and Helicopter Handling

Also available:

2nd Edition

THE
HELICOPTER
PILOT'S MANUAL

VOLUME 2

Powerplants, Instruments and Hydraulics

Norman Bailey

CONTENTS

INTRODUCTION

The whole process of learning to fly helicopters will be much easier if first you take the time to read about and understand the basic aerodynamic forces that act on a helicopter.

Helicopters lack the aerodynamic control feedback and built-in stability of fixed-wing aircraft. Flying them draws on a pilot's kinaesthetic senses and ability to extrapolate in four dimensions in real time. This is not something that can be learned overnight, but this book should help you progress more quickly through your initial training.

Few other books offer this combination of helicopter aerodynamic theory and practical hands-on advice in such an easy-to-read style. The first edition proved very popular and now is used by most helicopter training schools because of its simplified approach to learning to fly helicopters.

This new edition provides an update on current training rules and exercises while retaining the easily understood style.

Good luck with your flight training, and I hope you have many safe and enjoyable hours of helicopter flying.

Norman Bailey, DFM

1 THE PRINCIPLES OF HELICOPTER FLIGHT

Helicopters and other related rotary-wing aircraft are widely varied in their concept and configuration. This book concerns primarily the single-rotor helicopter, of the type that employs a compensating tail rotor.

Although the aerodynamics of the helicopter are based on the same laws that govern the flight of a fixed-wing aircraft, the significance of some considerations is somewhat different.

Both rely on lift produced from air flowing around an aerofoil, but whereas the aeroplane must move bodily forward through the air, the helicopter's rotors ('wings') move independently of the fuselage and can produce lift with the aircraft remaining stationary (hovering).

Both autogyros and helicopters have rotating wings (rotor blades), but those of the autogyro are not driven. Instead, they rotate freely in flight under the single influence of the airflow. The helicopter's rotor blades are engine driven in powered flight, giving it the ability to hover.

Before considering the principles of helicopter flight, it is necessary to explain some terms and definitions.

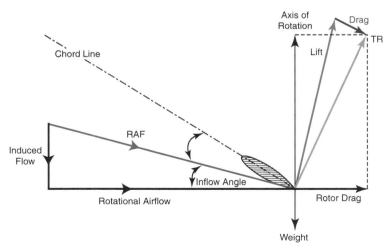

The principles of helicopter flight.

Aerofoil (*Airfoil in USA*) An aerofoil is any surface designed to produce lift when air passes over it. On a helicopter, the rotor blades are the aerofoils and normally are classed as symmetrical, because the blade's upper and lower surfaces have the same curvature.

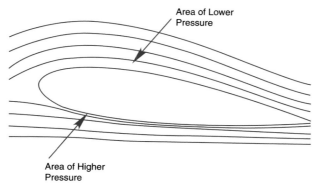

Aerofoil section.

Chord line This is an imaginary line joining a rotor blade's leading and trailing edges.

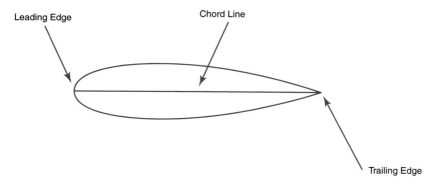

The chord line.

Axis of rotation An actual or imaginary line about which a body rotates.

Plane of rotation This is normal to the axis of rotation and parallel to the rotor tip-path plane. It is at right angles to the axis of rotation.

Tip-path plane The path described by the tips of the rotor blades as they rotate.

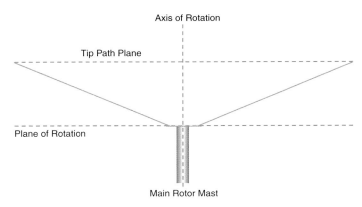

The tip-path plane.

The rotor disc The area contained by the tips of the rotor blades.

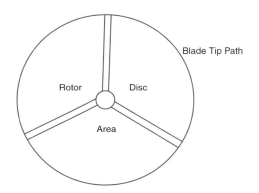

The rotor disc.

Pitch angle The angle between the chord line and the plane of rotation.

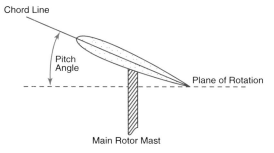

The pitch angle.

Coning angle The angle between the spanwise length of a rotor blade and its tip-path plane.

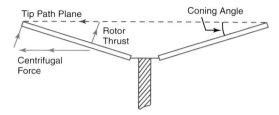

Coning angle.

Coning Movement of the rotor blades aligning them along the resultant of centrifugal force and lift. An increase in lift would increase the coning angle; conversely, an increase in rotor rpm would decrease the coning angle.

Feathering The angular movement of a rotor blade about its longitudinal axis.

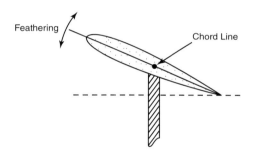

Feathering.

Flapping The angular movement of a rotor blade about a horizontal axis. In fully articulated rotors, the individual blades are free to flap about their flapping hinge.

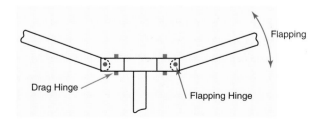

Flapping.

Dragging The angular movement of a rotor blade about an axis vertical to that blade. The dragging hinge is only incorporated in fully articulated rotor systems.

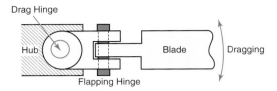

Dragging.

Angle of attack The angle between the chord line and the relative airflow.

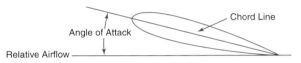

Angle of attack.

Total rotor thrust The sum of lift of all the rotor blades.

Disc loading The ratio of weight to the total main rotor-disc area.

Solidity ratio The ratio of the total blade area to the total disc area.

THE LIFTING FORCE OF THE ROTOR

Lift

To understand how lift is created, first we must review the basic principle of pressure differential. This was discovered by a Swiss physicist, Daniel Bernoulli. Simply put, Bernoulli's Principle states that as the velocity of a fluid (air) increases, its internal pressure decreases. When a relative wind blows across a rotor blade, the air divides, passing over the top of the blade and underneath it. Essentially, the air blowing across the top moves at a greater speed than that passing below, thereby creating a pressure differential, which results in lift.

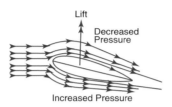

The pressure differential.

The lift produced from the wing of an aeroplane results from a combination of many things and commonly is expressed in the formula: $L = CL \frac{1}{2} pV^2 S$, where L = lift; CL = coefficient of lift; p = air density; V = velocity; and S = surface area of the blade.

Lift from a helicopter rotor blade can generally be expressed in the same terms, but because the rotor blade moves independently of the fuselage, the velocity (V2) when hovering in still-air conditions is purely the result of the rotation of the blade (rotor rpm).

Blade Pitch

The wing of an aeroplane is fitted to the fuselage at an angle, the datums being the chord line and a line running longitudinally down the fuselage. The angle between the two is known as the *angle of incidence*.

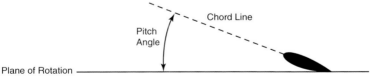

Blade pitch.

A rotor blade, when attached to the main rotor head, will also have a basic setting. The datums are the chord line of the rotor blade and the plane in which the rotor blade is free to rotate. This angle between the two datums is the *pitch angle*.

If the rotor blade had a constant value of pitch throughout its length, problems would arise in relation to blade loading, because each section of the blade would have a different rotational velocity and, therefore, a different value of lift. As lift is proportional to V2, if the speed were doubled, the lift would increase fourfold.

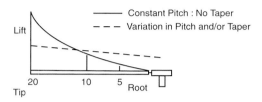

Blade lift.

To avoid this considerable variation of lift, it is necessary to increase lift at the root and decrease it at the tip. This can be achieved by tapering the blade, twisting the blade (washout), or a combination of the two. Even then, lift from the blade will have its greatest value near the tip, but its distribution along the blade will be more uniform.

Relative Airflow

Consider a column of still air through which a rotor blade is moving horizontally. The effect will be to displace some of the air downward. If a number of rotor blades are travelling along the same path in rapid succession (with a three-bladed rotor system operating at 240 rpm, a blade will be passing a given point every twelfth of a second), the column of still air will become a column of descending air.

Induced flow.

This column of descending air is known as the *induced flow*. Therefore, the direction of the air relative to the rotor blade will be the resultant of the blade's horizontal travel through the air and the induced flow.

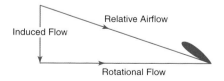

Relative airflow.

Total Reaction

This force acting on an aerofoil can be understood more easily if split into two components: lift and drag. Lift acts at a right angle to the relative airflow, but, as a result, does not provide a force in direct opposition to weight. Therefore, the lifting component of the total reaction must be the part that is acting along the axis of rotation. This component is known as *rotor thrust*. The other component of total reaction will be in the rotor blade's plane of rotation and is known as *rotor drag*.

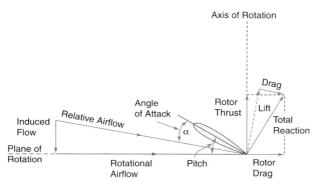

Total reaction.

Total Rotor Thrust

If the rotor blades are perfectly balanced and each blade is producing the same amount of rotor thrust, the *total rotor thrust* can be said to be acting through the rotor head at a right angle to the plane of rotation.

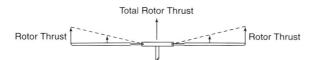

Total rotor thrust.

Coning Angle

The effect of rotor thrust will cause the rotor blades to rise until they reach a position where their upward movement is balanced by the outward pull of the centrifugal force generated by the rotation of the blades.

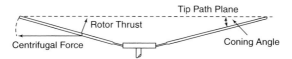

Coning angle.

At high rotor speeds, the blades produce a great deal of centrifugal force, keeping the coning angle low. When rotor speed is decreased, there is less centrifugal force, so the coning angle will increase. As this centrifugal action through rotor rpm gives a measure of control of the coning angle, provided the rotor speed is kept within the specified limits for a particular helicopter, the coning angle will remain within safe operating limits.

There will also be upper limits to the rotor rpm, due to engine and transmission considerations as well as end loading stresses where the blade is attached to the rotor head.

HELICOPTER SYSTEMS

There are many variations in the design of a modern helicopter. Even though helicopters come in all shapes and sizes, however, they share many of the same major components.

Flight Control Systems
Main Rotor Systems
Main rotor systems are classified according to how the rotor blades move relative to the main rotor hub. The main categories are fully articulated, semi-rigid and rigid.

Fully articulated Each main rotor blade is free to move up and down (flapping), to move back and forth (dragging), and to twist about the spanwise axis (feathering). This type of system normally has three or more blades.

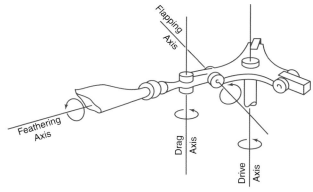

Fully articulated rotor system.

Semi-rigid system Normally, two main rotor blades are rigidly attached to the main rotor hub, which is free to tilt and rock independently of the main rotor mast on what is known as a teetering hinge – as one blade flaps up, the other flaps down. There is no vertical drag hinge.

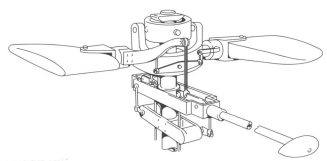

Semi-rigid rotor system.

Rigid rotor system This system, although mechanically simple, is structurally complex because the operating loads must be absorbed by bending rather than through hinges. The rotor blades cannot flap or drag, but can be feathered. The natural frequency of the rigid rotor is so high that air and ground resonance are less of a problem. What is a problem, though, is that the control loads are high, making stability difficult to achieve.

Anti-torque Systems
Most single-rotor helicopters require a separate rotor to overcome the effect of torque reaction, i.e. the tendency for the helicopter to turn in the opposite direction to that of the main rotor blades.

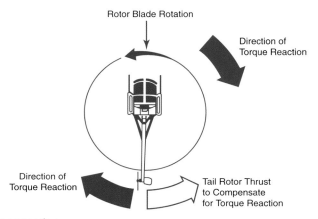

Torque compensation.

Another form of anti-torque rotor is the *Fenestron*, often called 'the fan in the tail' rotor. This system employs a series of rotating blades shrouded within the vertical tail fin of the helicopter. Because the blades operate inside the ducted area, they are protected from contacting external objects.

Fenestron tail rotor.

18

Finally, there is the *NOTAR* (no tail rotor) system, an alternative to the anti-torque rotor. This design uses low-pressure air forced into the tail cone by an internal fan. The pressurized air is fed through horizontal slots and a controllable rotating nozzle to provide anti-torque and directional control.

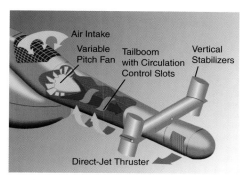

NOTAR anti-torque system.

Twin-rotor helicopters do not require a separate anti-torque rotor because the torque from one rotor is balanced by the torque from the other, thereby cancelling out the turning tendency.

Landing Gear

Skids The most common type of helicopter undercarriage, skids are suitable for landing on all types of surface. Some are fitted with dampers so that touchdown shocks are not transmitted to the main rotor system. Skids not fitted with dampers absorb such shocks by allowing the cross-tube to flex. Small wheels fitted to the skids can be lowered to facilitate movement of the helicopter on the ground.

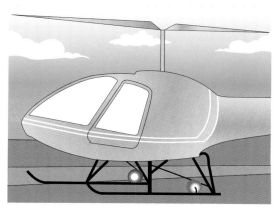

Landing skids.

Wheels Usually found on large helicopters, wheels may be fitted in a three- or four-wheel configuration. Normally, the nose wheel is free to swivel as the helicopter is taxied on the ground. To reduce drag in flight, some designs allow the wheels to retract.

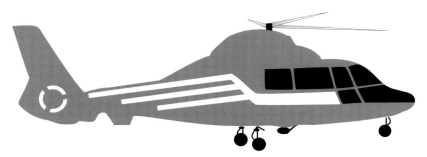

Wheel landing gear.

Flotation Many helicopters can be fitted with floatation bags for operations over water. There are two basic types of floatation gear: pontoon floats that replace the skids and are permanently inflated; and pop-out floats that can be inflated in an emergency, either automatically or by the pilot.

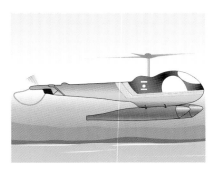

Pontoon floats.

Pop-out floats.

Operation of Flight Control Systems
A knowledge of the flight control systems is necessary, as by understanding their operation, you will be able to recognize potential problems when conducting your pre-flight inspection.

Collective Pitch Control (Lever)
Usually operated by the pilot's left hand, the collective pitch lever controls the lift produced by the rotor. Movement of the lever simultaneously adjusts the pitch of all the blades by the same amount.

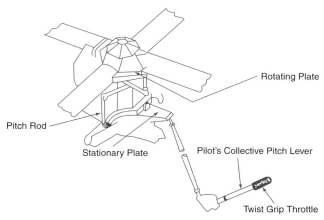

Collective pitch control system.

Cyclic Pitch Control (Stick)
Usually operated by the pilot's right hand the cyclic pitch control changes the pitch angle of the rotor blades in their cyclic rotation. This tilts the main rotor tip-path plane to allow forward, rearward or lateral movement of the helicopter.

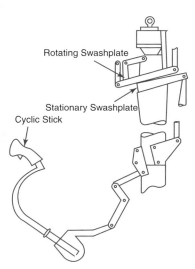

Cyclic pitch control system.

Anti-Torque Control (Pedals)
The anti-torque pedals are operated by the pilot's feet and vary the force produced by the tail rotor to oppose torque reaction. When you apply left pedal, you increase the pitch of the tail rotor blades, which increases the thrust to the right and moves the nose of the helicopter to the left.

Swash Plate Assembly
The purpose of the swash plate is to transmit cyclic and collective control movements to the main rotor blades. In its simplest form, it consists of a stationary plate and a rotating plate. The stationary plate is attached to the main rotor mast and, although restricted from rotating, is allowed to tilt in all directions and move vertically. The rotating plate is attached to the stationary plate by a bearing surface and rotates at the same speed as the main rotor blades. It transmits pitch changes through mechanical linkages. Cyclic pitch changes tilt the rotating plate and alter the main rotor blade pitch through the pitch control arms. Collective pitch changes are made by moving the whole swash plate bodily up and down while maintaining the angle of tilt.

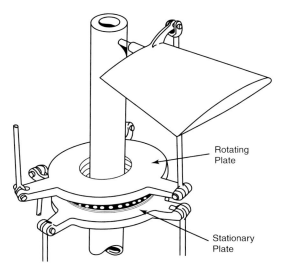

Swash plate assembly.

Trim
Many helicopters are equipped with some form of trim arrangement to relieve the pilot from having to hold the controls against any forces in the system. The neutral position of the cyclic stick changes as the helicopter moves off from the hover into forward flight. The control feel in a helicopter is provided mechanically, and you can adjust this mechanical feel in flight by changing the neutral position of the stick using the trim control.

Frictions
Since the main rotor blades tend to feed back aerodynamic forces to the pilot's controls, trim springs are used to resist any control motion. Friction controls provide adjustable resistance to control movements.

The Power Train

On a piston-engined helicopter, the power train usually consists of a clutch, main rotor transmission and drive, a tail rotor transmission and drive, and a freewheel unit to allow the rotors to turn freely in the event of an engine failure.

Engine

A typical light helicopter is usually powered by an air-cooled piston engine mounted behind the cabin. A fan is employed to assist engine cooling. This can absorb up to 10 per cent of engine power in the hover.

Clutch

In an aeroplane, the engine and propeller are permanently engaged, but because of the greater weight of the helicopter's rotor system in relation to engine power, a piston-engined helicopter is usually started with the rotors disconnected from the engine to relieve the load. Even more important, there must be some way to disconnect the engine from the rotors in case of engine failure, since otherwise the rotor would stop with the engine.

Some helicopters use a centrifugal-type clutch, in which contact between the inner and outer parts is made by spring-loaded brake shoes. At low engine speeds, the clutch shoes are held out of contact by springs. As engine speed increases, centrifugal force throws the clutch shoes outward until they contact the clutch drum.

Many helicopters utilize a form of belt drive to transmit engine power to the main rotor transmission. Normally, this consists of a lower pulley attached to the engine crankshaft, an upper pulley attached to the input shaft of the main gearbox, an idler pulley and belt(s). Tension on the belt(s) is gradually increased to regulate the rate of rotor engagement.

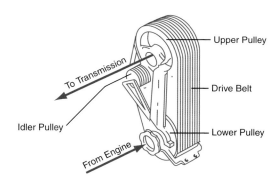

Belt drive.

Freewheel

All helicopters are designed so that the main rotors can be disengaged from the engine in the event of a power failure. In helicopters with a belt drive system, this is achieved by means of a freewheel unit (one-way sprag clutch) contained in the upper pulley. When the engine is driving the rotor, inclined surfaces force rollers against the outer drum. If the engine fails, the rollers move inward, allowing the outer drum to continue turning.

Tail Rotor Drive System
A tail rotor driveshaft, powered from the main transmission, is connected to the tail rotor transmission located on the end of the tail cone. The tail rotor transmission provides a right-angle drive and gears to increase the input speed so that the output shaft rotates at optimum tail rotor rpm. The tail gearbox is splash lubricated from its own oil supply. You can check the oil level by means of a sight glass or plug.

HELICOPTER CONTROLS

A helicopter is able to climb and descend vertically, move horizontally in any direction and, while hovering above a spot on the ground, turn on to any selected heading. To achieve this variety of performance, the helicopter is fitted with special controls.

Collective Pitch Control (Lever)

This control gets its name from the fact that when it is raised, it simultaneously increases the pitch angles of all the rotor blades equally. Similarly, when it is lowered, it reduces their pitch angles equally. These changes are called *collective pitch movements*.

The first requirement is to be able to control the amount of total rotor thrust. We have said already that this force depends on angle of attack, airspeed and size/shape of the aerofoil (rotor blade). The last two can be disregarded, since they are design features. The airspeed of a rotor blade is governed by the speed of rotation, which, in the modern helicopter, is virtually constant, the maximum and minimum limitations being quite close together.

Limits of Rotor Speed

The maximum rotor speed is governed by such factors as maximum engine rpm (piston engine) and transmission limitations (gas-turbine engine). Since the gap between maximum and minimum rotor rpm is so small, there can be no question of varying the speed to control the amount of total rotor thrust. In any case, the response would be too slow because of the considerable inertia of the rotor blades. It follows that the only practical means of control is by varying the angle of attack of the blades, which is done by means of the collective pitch control (lever).

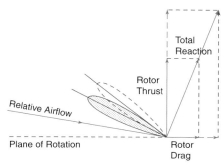

Control of rotor rpm.

Pitch Angle

Variations in blade pitch will cause marked changes in drag, and to maintain constant rotor rpm, changes in power must be made. This is achieved by having a throttle control on the end of the lever.

Cyclic Pitch Control (Stick)

To move the helicopter into horizontal flight, a thrust force is required, which must be produced by the main rotor. This can be achieved by tilting the rotor disc so that the total rotor thrust is angled in the direction of the required movement.

In the case of a two-bladed rotor, if the pitch of one blade is increased while that of the other is decreased by the same amount at the same time, one blade will rise and the other will fall, resulting in the rotor disc being tilted. To keep the rotor disc tilted, the pitch must vary throughout the blades' 360-degree cycle of travel. This changing pitch is known as *cyclic pitch* and is achieved by the pilot moving the stick.

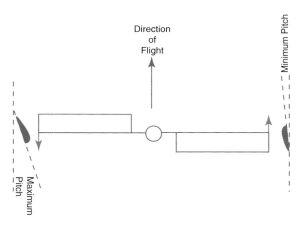

Cyclic pitch.

Torque Reaction

Unless balanced in some way, the fuselage will rotate in the opposite direction to the main rotor as a result of *torque reaction*. As mentioned, the most common method used to overcome this is by fitting a tail rotor.

As torque reaction is not a constant – it varies with power changes – some means must be provided to vary the thrust of the tail rotor. This is achieved by the pilot moving the pedals, which collectively change the pitch, and thereby angle of attack, of the tail rotor blades. The pitch increases or decreases depending on which pedal is moved. When tail rotor thrust equals torque reaction, the helicopter will maintain a constant heading.

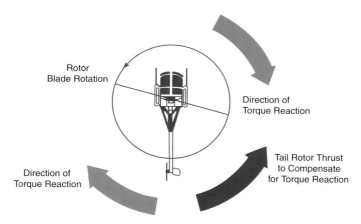

Torque reaction.

Additional Functions of the Tail Rotor

Changing heading in the hover By operating the pedals to produce a thrust greater or less than torque reaction, the pilot can alter the heading of the helicopter while hovering over a ground position. The pedals operate in the correct sense, in that a yaw to the right results from pushing on the right pedal, and vice versa.

To maintain a balanced condition in forward flight By using the pedals to keep the balance indicator centralised, the pilot can ensure that the helicopter flies straight.

To prevent the fuselage from rotating in autorotation When the rotors are being turned purely by the reaction to the air and without assistance from the engine, friction will cause the fuselage to rotate in the same direction as the main rotor.

The tail rotor blades are symmetrical in shape and must be capable of being turned to produce plus or minus values in pitch angle.

Tail Rotor Drift

Consider a bar that is being turned under the influence of a couple, YY, about a point X. The rotation will stop if a couple of equal value, ZZ, pulls in the opposite direction.

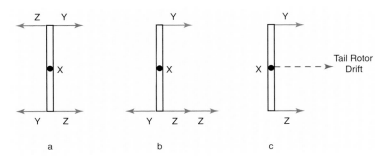

Tail rotor drift.

The rotation would also stop if a single force were used to produce a moment equal to the couple, YY, but there would now be a side loading on the pivot point, X.

The tail rotor of a helicopter produces a moment to overcome the couple arising from torque reaction, which in turn causes a side loading on the axis of rotation (pivot point) of the main rotor. This side loading is known as *tail rotor drift*, and unless corrected it would result in the helicopter moving sideways over the ground.

Since the value of a moment is the product of force multiplied by distance, the greater the distance that the tail rotor acts from the main rotor's axis of rotation, the smaller the force required. In practice, the tail rotor is normally positioned just clear of the main rotor.

Tail rotor drift can be corrected by tilting the rotor disc away from the direction of drift.

This can be achieved by:

- The pilot moving the cyclic stick.
- Rigging the controls so that when the cyclic is in the centre, the disc is actually tilted by the right amount.
- Mounting the engine so that the drive shaft to the rotor is offset.
- Causing the disc to tilt when the collective lever is raised.

Tail Rotor Roll

If the tail rotor is mounted on the fuselage below the level of the main rotor, the force produced by the main rotor to correct tail rotor drift will create a rolling couple with the tail rotor thrust, causing the helicopter to hover one skid low. This can be overcome if the tail rotor is raised to the level of the main rotor by cranking the fuselage or fitting the tail rotor to a pylon. This condition will only be achieved, however, if the helicopter is loaded with the *centre of gravity* (CG) in the ideal position. A helicopter is usually designed so that the tail rotor is level with the main rotor at cruising speeds.

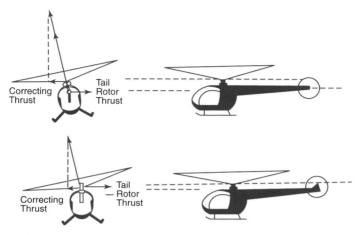

Tail rotor roll.

The conventional tail rotor operates in difficult aerodynamic conditions and is susceptible to damage by foreign objects. Also, it is a danger to ground personnel. One solution to these disadvantages is the shrouded, or Fenestron, tail rotor, where the rotor blades are hinged about their feathering axis only and operate within a shroud on the tail fin.

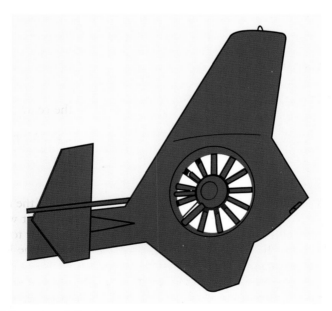

Shrouded Fenestron tail rotor.

ROTOR FREEDOM OF MOVEMENT

Feathering

This describes the movement of the main rotor blade relative to its plane of rotation. Feathering takes place as a result of changes in collective or cyclic pitch.

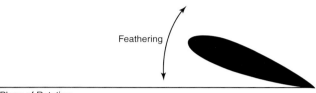

Feathering.

Flapping

This describes the movement of the rotor blade perpendicular to the main hub. Flapping occurs as a result of collective and cyclic pitch changes, variations in rotor rpm, and changes in speed and direction of airflow relative to the disc, which happen in certain flight conditions.

To alleviate bending stresses that otherwise would occur, the rotor blade is allowed to move about a flapping hinge. In some helicopters, the rotor blades are allowed to see-saw about the rotor hub.

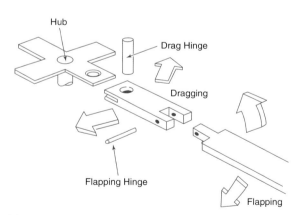

Flapping hinge assembly.

Dragging

This describes the freedom given to each rotor blade to allow it to move in the plane of rotation independently of the other blades. To avoid bending stresses at the root, the blade is permitted to drag about a dragging hinge. Such movement is retarded by some form of drag damper to prevent undesirable oscillations.

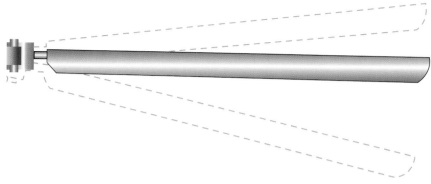

Rotor blade dragging.

Dragging occurs because of:

Periodic drag changes When the helicopter moves horizontally, each rotor blade's angle of attack is continually changing during each revolution to provide asymmetry of rotor thrust. This variation in angle of attack results in a variation of rotor drag; consequently, the rotor blade will lead or lag about the dragging hinge.

Changing position of the blade CG relative to the rotor hub Consider the helicopter stationary on the ground in still-air conditions, with the rotors turning. The radius of the blades' CG relative to the axis of rotation will be constant.

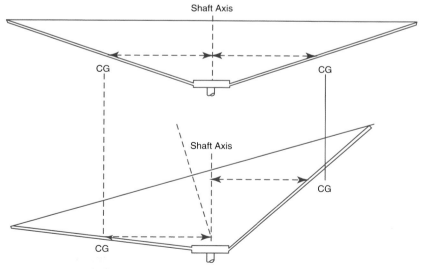

Changing position of blade CG.

If the cyclic stick is moved, the rotor blade will flap up on one side and down on the other to produce a change in disc attitude. With the helicopter stationary on the ground, the axis about which the blades are turning will not have altered, so the radius of the blades' CG relative to the axis will be changing continuously through each 360 degrees of travel.

This variation in radius will cause the blade to speed up or slow down about the dragging hinge, depending upon whether the radius is increasing or decreasing. This is known as the *Coriolis Effect*, and it will also occur when the helicopter first moves into horizontal flight.

Hooke's Joint Effect This effect is difficult to describe, but basically it is the movement of the rotor blade to reposition itself relative to the other rotor blades when cyclic pitch is applied. The effect is very similar to the movement of the rotor blades' CG relative to the main rotor hub.

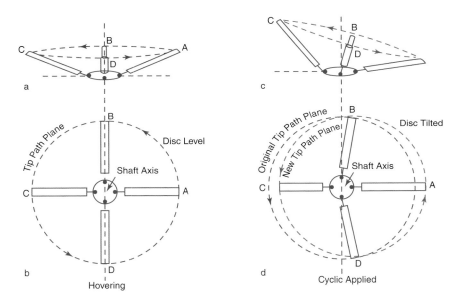

Hooke's Joint Effect.

Consider the rotor of a helicopter hovering in still air. When viewed from above the shaft axis, rotor blades A, B, C and D appear equally spaced. When a cyclic tilt of the disc occurs, the cone axis tilts, but if still viewed from above the shaft axis, which has not tilted, blade A will appear to increase its radius, and blade C to decrease its radius. Blades B and D must maintain position to achieve their true radial locations on the cone. It follows, therefore, that they must move in the plane of rotation and position themselves accordingly.

FLAPPING TO EQUALITY

Moving the cyclic stick does not alter the magnitude of total rotor thrust, but simply changes the disc attitude. This is achieved by the rotor blades *flapping to equality*. Consider a rotor blade on a helicopter in the hover where the angle of attack is 6 degrees. A cyclic movement decreases the blade pitch and, assuming initially the direction of the relative airflow remains unchanged, the reduction in pitch will reduce both the blade's angle of attack and rotor thrust.

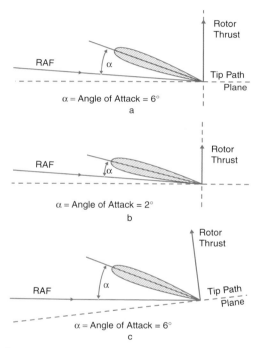

Flapping to equality.

The blade will now begin to flap down, causing an automatic increase in the blade's angle of attack. When the angle of attack reaches 6 degrees again, rotor thrust will return to its original value and the blade will continue to follow a path to maintain a constant angle of attack. Thus, cyclic pitch will alter the plane in which the blade rotates, but the angle of attack remains unchanged.

The reverse occurs when a rotor blade is subject to an increase in cyclic pitch.

Therefore, any change in angle of attack through control action or in-flight conditions causes the rotor blades to flap, and they will do so until they restore the rotor thrust – they have then *flapped to equality*.

PHASE LAG AND ADVANCE ANGLE

Control Orbit

In its simplest form of operation, movement of the collective pitch lever causes a flat plate mounted centrally on the main rotor mast to rise and fall. Movement of the cyclic stick causes the plate to tilt in the direction in which the cyclic stick is moved.

Rods of equal length, called *pitch operating arms*, connect the flat plate to the rotor blades. When the plate is tilted, the pitch operating arms move up or down, increasing or decreasing the pitch of the main rotor blades.

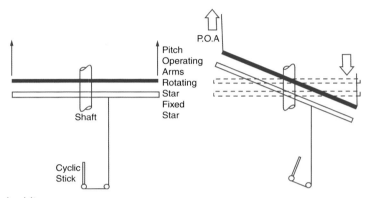

Control orbit.

The flat plate can be more accurately described as a *control orbit*, because it represents the plane in which the pitch operating arms rotate.

Pitch Operating Arm Movement

Consider now the effect of the movement of a pitch operating arm when the control orbit is tilted 2 degrees. (It is assumed that the control orbit tilts in the same direction in which the stick is moved.) If the movement of the pitch operating arm through 360 degrees of travel is plotted on a simple graph, the result will be as shown below.

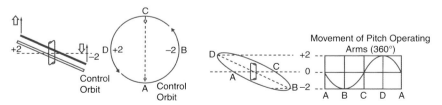

Pitch operating arm movement.   Travel of pitch operating arm.

Resultant Change in Disc Attitude
The rotor blades will respond to the cyclic pitch change by flapping, and the resultant change in disc attitude can be determined by following the movement of each blade of a two-bladed rotor system.

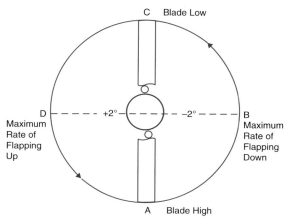

Change in disc attitude.

Consider the rotor blades to be positioned at A and C when the control orbit is tilted; the pitch operating arms are attached to the control orbit directly beneath the rotor blades. As the blade moves anti-clockwise from A, it will undergo a reduction in pitch, and the blade will flap down. The rate of flapping varies with the amount of pitch change, so the blade will experience its greatest rate of flapping down as it passes position B (maximum pitch change). In the next 90 degrees of travel, the pitch will return from –2 degrees to zero, so the rate of flapping will have died out by position C. The blade that started at position A will flap down for 180 degrees of travel and, therefore, will reach a low position at C.

The reverse will take place with the other blade, which will reach a high position at A. Now the disc will be tilted along the axis BD, 90 degrees removed from the tilt axis of the control orbit.

Phase Lag
When cyclic pitch is applied, the rotor blades will automatically flap to equality. In doing so, the disc attitude will change, the blade reaching its highest and lowest position 90 degrees later than the point where it experiences the maximum increase and decrease of cyclic pitch. The variation between the tilt of the control orbit and the subsequent tilt of the rotor disc is known as *phase lag*.

Advance Angle

If the control orbit tilts in the same direction as the cyclic stick and, as a result, the disc tilts 90 degrees out of phase with the control orbit, the disc will also tilt 90 degrees out of phase with the cyclic stick. Thus, unless the system is compensated in some way, moving the cyclic stick forward would cause the helicopter to move sideways.

One way to overcome this problem is to arrange for the rotor blade to receive the maximum alteration in cyclic pitch 90 degrees before the blade is over the highest and lowest points on the control orbit. Another way would be to make the control orbit tilt so that it is out of phase with the cyclic stick by the required angle.

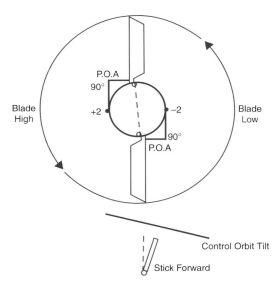

Advance angle.

The angular distance that the pitch operating arm is positioned on the control orbit, in advance of the rotor blade to which it relates, is known as the *advance angle*.

HOVERING

Take-Off to the Hover

To lift the helicopter off the ground, a lifting force must be produced that is equal and opposite to the weight that suspends vertically through the helicopter's centre of gravity.

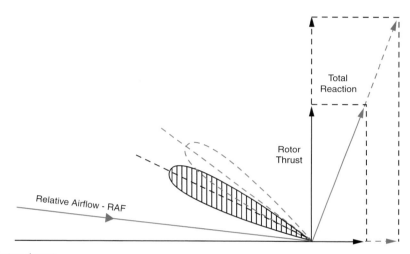

Rotor thrust.

When the rotor is turning at flying rpm, with the collective lever fully down, very little rotor thrust will be produced. As the collective lever is raised, the rotor blades will begin to cone up, and eventually the rotor thrust will equal the helicopter's weight. If the collective lever is raised further, the rotor thrust will increase yet more, and when it becomes greater than the helicopter's weight, the helicopter will accelerate upward. After a short time, the acceleration will become a steady rate of climb, and the helicopter will continue in this state until the pilot lowers the collective lever.

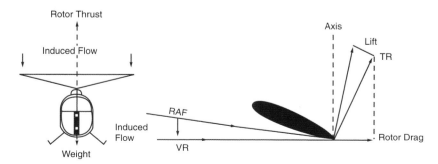

Take-off to the hover.

Consider the helicopter to be 200 ft above the ground when the collective lever is lowered slightly to stop it from climbing further. The helicopter will now come to the hover. Being well clear of the ground, this condition is known as a *free air hover* (hover out of ground effect).

Vertical Descent and Climb

If the collective lever is lowered in the free air hover, the angle of attack will reduce, rotor thrust will become less than weight, and the helicopter will begin to accelerate downward. The airflow resulting from the helicopter's descent will oppose the induced flow and cause the angle of attack to increase. When it reaches its original value, rotor thrust will equal weight and the downward acceleration will become a steady rate of descent.

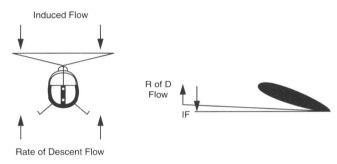

Vertical descent.

In a vertical climb, the reverse takes place. Increased collective pitch raises the angle of attack, rotor thrust becomes greater than weight, and the helicopter accelerates upward. The airflow from the rate of climb is in the same direction as the induced flow, and the resultant change in airflow direction to the rotor blades will gradually reduce the angle of attack. Again, when it reaches its original value, rotor thrust equals weight and the upward acceleration will become a steady rate of climb.

Ground Cushion Effect

In a free air hover, the resistance to the induced flow is only the resistance of the surrounding air. In a hover close to the ground, the ground itself will resist the induced flow. This will be at a maximum when hovering just above the surface. The ground effect intensifies the pressure differential around the rotor. Accelerated air, having passed through the rotor disc, strikes the ground and is slowed down, which increases the pressure under the rotor. This, in turn, causes a reduction in the induced flow and a consequent increase in angle of attack.

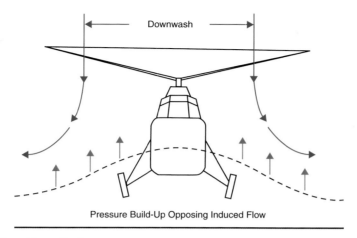

Ground cushion effect.

Therefore, the same angle of attack can be maintained in ground effect (IGE) with less collective pitch and power than would be required out of ground effect (OGE). This reduction in power is possible because of a reduction in rotor drag.

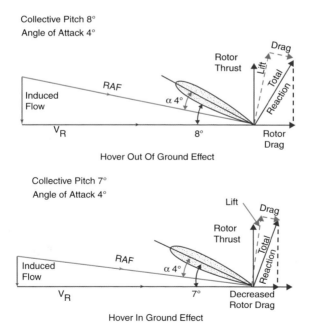

Hovering and ground effect.

Factors that Affect Ground Cushion
Several factors affect the ground cushion:

- The height the helicopter is hovering above the ground. Ground cushion effect disappears at a height equal to about three-quarters of the diameter of the rotor disc. The lower the hover height, the more intense the ground effect.
- Nature of the ground. Rough ground dissipates the cushion; long grass absorbs the cushion. Concrete and tarmac surfaces produce the best effects.
- Sloping ground. This makes for an uneven ground cushion.
- Wind velocity. The cushion is displaced downwind. Hovering into wind places the cushion nicely underneath the helicopter.

Recirculation
Whenever a helicopter is hovering close to the ground, some of the air passing through the rotor disc is recirculated, and it would appear that the recirculated air increases in speed as it passes through a second time. This local increase in induced flow near the rotor blade tips gives rise to a loss of rotor thrust.

Some recirculation always takes place, but over a flat, even surface, the loss of rotor thrust to recirculation is more than counteracted by the ground cushion effect. If the helicopter is hovering over long grass, the loss of lift due to recirculation will increase, and in some cases, the effect will be greater than the ground cushion. When this situation arises, more power is required to hover near the ground than to hover in free air.

Recirculation will increase when any obstruction on the surface, or near to where the helicopter is hovering, prevents the air from flowing away evenly. This can be dangerous, especially if it develops on only one side of the rotor disc.

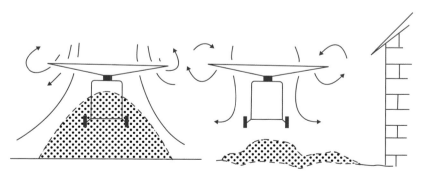

Recirculation.

Never hover within one rotor diameter of a building or another helicopter measured from the rotor tips.

POWER

Power is defined as the *rate* of doing *work*.

$$\text{Therefore, Power} = \frac{\text{Work}}{\text{Time}} = \frac{\text{Drag} \times \text{Distance}}{\text{Time}}$$

$$\text{But} \quad \frac{\text{Distance}}{\text{Time}} = \text{Velocity}$$

Therefore, Power = Drag × Velocity.

Power is normally expressed in terms of horsepower, one horsepower being equal to 550 ft/lb/sec or 33,000 ft/lb/min.

When an object is moved, *force* is required to overcome its resistance. If the force is multiplied by the *distance* the object is moved, the product is the amount of *work* done.

The resistance set up by the rotor blades as they turn through the air is called *drag*. Since in any balanced equation, force equals drag, then work must be equal to drag multiplied by distance.

The resistance or drag of a body moving through the air will vary as the *square* of the speed, but the power required to balance the drag will vary as the *cube* of the speed.

Power Required

The power required to maintain level flight throughout a helicopter's speed range can be considered under three main headings:

Parasite power This is the power required to overcome the drag of the fuselage when the helicopter is moving in straight and level flight.

Rotor profile power The power component related to the rotor blade's speed for a fixed value of drag is known as rotor profile power. The drag value will be at a minimum with the collective pitch lever fully down, and will increase as the lever is raised. When the main rotor is turning, however, ancillary equipment, drive shafts and the tail rotor will also be absorbing power. All these power requirements must be included when calculating rotor profile power.

As forward speed increases, the power required to maintain rotor rpm will increase. The reason for this is because in forward flight, the increase in drag of the advancing blade will be greater than the decrease in drag of the retreating blade.

Rotor profile power accounts for about 40 per cent of the power required to hover.

Induced power When the collective pitch lever is fully down, virtually no rotor thrust is produced. To increase rotor thrust, the lever must be raised, but this will give rise to:

1. An increase in rotor drag.
2. An increase in the mass of air flowing down through the rotor disc.

To maintain a constant rotor rpm, more power must be applied to balance the increasing drag of the rotor blades. This increase in power is known as induced power, because it is the extra power required to overcome the rise in drag when the rotor blades are inducing airflow down through the rotor.

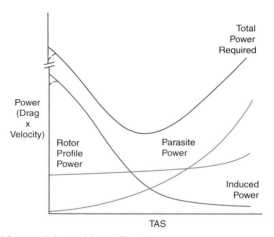

Power required for straight and level flight.

Induced power accounts for about 60 per cent of the power required to hover.

The power required to maintain the helicopter in straight and level flight at any given forward speed is the combination of rotor profile power, induced power and parasite power.

Power Available

The efficiency of the helicopter's main rotor system is taken into account in assessing the power required for straight and level flight. Therefore, power available is the power supplied *to* the main rotor and not *from* it. For any given altitude, this power will remain more or less constant, so it appears as a straight line on the power graph.

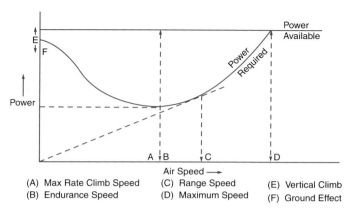

(A) Max Rate Climb Speed   (C) Range Speed   (E) Vertical Climb
(B) Endurance Speed   (D) Maximum Speed   (F) Ground Effect

Power available.

The maximum forward speed will be where the two curves cross. The speed to give maximum rate of climb will be where the two curves are furthest apart; the greater the power available, the faster the rate of climb. Range speed will be where a line drawn from the graph point of origin touches the 'power required' curve at a tangent. (This is true for piston-engined helicopters only – range speed for gas-turbine helicopters is appreciably higher.) Endurance speed will be the speed for minimum power, the lowest point on the 'power required' curve.

Factors Affecting Power Available/Power Required
Power Available
In a piston-engined helicopter, power available is affected by air density and altitude changes. This can be compensated for turbocharging.

Power Required
The power required by the main rotor is affected by air density and all-up weight. Consider a helicopter hovering outside ground effect (OGE). If rotor speed is maintained as height is increased, rotor profile power will decrease because of the reduction in air density. If total rotor thrust is to be maintained, the collective pitch lever must be raised to compensate for this density change and, therefore, the induced power must increase, eventually leading to the 'total power required' curve moving up the graph.

Weight
Any increase in weight will require a greater total rotor thrust, and for a given rotor speed this can only be achieved by raising the collective pitch lever. Therefore, the helicopter will reach the height at which it will produce its optimum rotor blade setting sooner than if it were lightly laden.

LIMITED POWER

Changes in air density, altitude and all-up weight will cause the 'power available' and 'power required' curves to move closer together. Eventually, power available may be sufficient to hover only in ground effect, and in extreme conditions, there may be insufficient power to hover at all.

Rarely are conditions the same at the take-off and landing points. In order that the pilot may make an assessment of the power available before committing to a landing, a simple in-flight power check can be carried out. When flying straight and level at some pre-determined airspeed (usually around the 40 mph mark), a note is made of the power (manifold pressure) required. Full power is then applied while maintaining rotor rpm to establish maximum power available. The difference between the two readings is the *power margin*, and it is this that determines the type of landing technique that can be carried out safely.

A similar type of power check can be made to assess the helicopter's take-off capability while in the hover before transitioning away.

These calculations do not allow for any wind effect, this being considered a bonus.

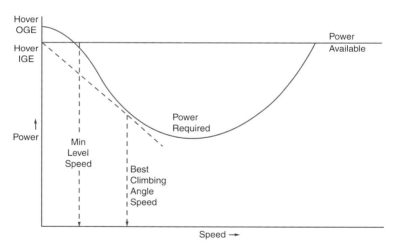

Limited power.

Best Climbing Angle

When operating with limited power, the helicopter must be moving forward to be able to climb. To assess the steepest climbing angle, it is necessary to find the best rate of climb/forward speed ratio. This can be determined by drawing a line from the point where the 'power available' curve cuts the vertical axis of the graph tangential to the 'power required' curve. Where the two lines touch is the speed for the maximum climbing angle. This point indicates the best ratio of power margin for climbing against minimum forward speed and, therefore, the steepest angle. It will always be less than the maximum rate of climb speed.

Turning

As well as providing a component to balance weight and a force to maintain speed, the total rotor thrust must also supply a further component to change the direction of the helicopter in a balanced turn. Its effect is similar to an increase in all-up weight. In a 30-degree-bank turn, the apparent increase in weight is 15 per cent; in a 60-degree-bank turn, it is 100 per cent.

To maintain height in the turn, more collective pitch is required. Therefore, more power is used, which causes the 'power required' curve to move up the graph.

The maximum angle of bank that can be achieved by a helicopter in a level turn is the angle where the airspeed is the speed for maximum rate of climb. If the angle of bank is increased beyond this point, height will be lost and rotor speed will decay.

Overpitching

High pitch angles cause high rotor drag, which means more power will be required to maintain a constant rotor speed. If the extra power is not available, rotor rpm will decay and the rotor blades cone upward. The disc area will decrease, more pitch will be required, and the rotor rpm will reduce further. This situation is called *overpitching* and is dangerous, because the only corrective action is to lower the collective lever and reduce the pitch angle, which in turn leads to a loss of height.

Overpitching is usually caused by mishandling the collective lever without a correct corresponding throttle movement. In this situation, the throttle should be opened to restore rotor rpm; if necessary, the collective lever should be lowered.

FORWARD FLIGHT

Symmetry of Rotor Thrust

If a helicopter is stationary on the ground in still-air conditions, with rotors turning, and some collective pitch is applied, the rotor thrust produced by each blade will be the same. The speed of the relative airflow over each rotor blade will be equal to the speed of rotation of the blades.

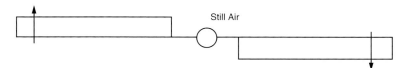

Symmetry of rotor thrust.

Dissymmetry of Rotor Thrust

If the conditions change and the helicopter now faces into a wind, during a blade's rotation through 360 degrees, half the time, it will be moving into the wind, and half the time with the wind. Therefore, the rotor disc can be divided into *advancing* and *retreating* sides.

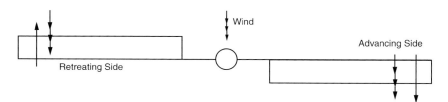

Dissymmetry of rotor thrust.

The value of rotor thrust across the disc will no longer be uniform, and unless some method is employed to compensate for this, the helicopter will roll toward the retreating side.

This condition, where one side of the disc has more rotor thrust than the other, is known as *dissymmetry of rotor thrust*.

Flapback

To maintain control of the helicopter, it is obvious that dissymmetry must not be allowed to take place. One method of preventing it is to decrease the angle of attack on the advancing blade, and increase the angle on the retreating blade, so that each rotor blade produces the same value of rotor thrust. With a fully articulated rotor head, this change in angle of attack takes place automatically, but in so doing, results in a change of disc attitude.

As the blade begins to travel on the advancing side, the relative airflow will increase. Rotor thrust increases and the blade flaps up, the maximum rate of flapping occurring at point A in the illustration below. For the next 90 degrees of travel, the velocity of the relative airflow begins to decrease, so the rate of flapping decreases.

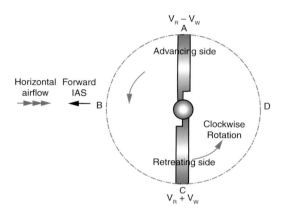

Flapback.

When the blade reaches point B, relative airflow will have the same value as at point D, so the rate of flapping dies out, but because the blade has been rising all the time since point D, it will reach its highest point at B.

The reverse will take place on the retreating side, the blade having its maximum rate of flapping down at point C, and reaching its lowest position at point D.

Therefore, the rotor disc will have flapped away from the wind. This change of disc attitude, which has occurred without any control movement, is known as *flapback*.

Factors Affecting Maximum Forward Speed

Cyclic Stick Design Limits

To initiate forward flight, the pilot moves the cyclic stick forward to tilt the main rotor disc. The disc tilts by the same amount that the stick has been moved. As the helicopter starts to travel forward, the cyclic stick has to be moved further forward to overcome the effects of flapback. Thus, a speed could be reached where all the cyclic stick movement has been used up to correct for flapback, with nothing left to increase forward speed further.

Airflow Reversal

The speed of rotation of the retreating main rotor blade is high at the tip and low at the root. The airflow from forward flight will have an equal value for the whole length of the rotor blade. As a result, the velocity of the relative airflow along the rotor blade will vary, and where the airflow from forward flight is greater than the blade's rotational velocity, the airflow will be from behind the rotor blade.

Although this does not have a direct effect on the maximum forward speed (Vne), it does mean that the cyclic stick will have to be used to correct the change in rotor disc attitude that otherwise would occur.

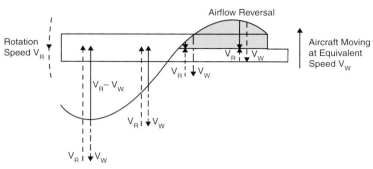

Airflow reversal.

Retreating Blade Stall

To counter airflow reversal, the retreating blade must operate at a higher angle of attack, the angle being greatest when the rotor blade is half-way around on the retreating side. As the helicopter's forward speed increases, so the retreating blade's angle of attack must increase. Eventually, a forward speed will be reached where the retreating rotor blade will stall. The loss in rotor thrust will cause the blade to flap down, but instead of flapping to equality, the blade will simply stall even further, starting at the tip and spreading inboard.

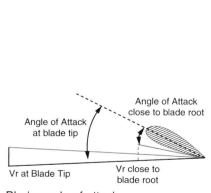

Blade angle of attack.

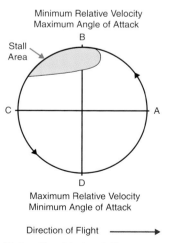

Retreating blade stall.

Compressibility
The rotational velocity at the rotor blade tip can be as high as 400–500 mph. When the helicopter is in forward flight, the additional velocity over the advancing rotor blade will increase the relative airflow by an amount equal to the forward speed. Because the rotor blades are designed mainly for low speeds, compressibility effects become apparent at a relatively low forward speed. The rise in rotor blade drag resulting from compressibility effects will require higher power to maintain rotor rpm, and cyclic stick correction to control disc attitude. It will have a maximum effect when the advancing rotor blade is half-way between the rear and front of the disc.

Limits of Cyclic Stick Imposed by All-Up Weight, Altitude and CG
The more heavily a helicopter is loaded, the greater must be the angle of attack to produce the necessary rotor thrust. Therefore, the retreating blade will reach its stalling angle at a lower forward speed with a higher all-up weight than when it the helicopter is lightly laden. As forward speed is a function of cyclic stick, there will be a limit on the movement of the stick imposed by the speed at which the retreating blade will stall.

To hover a helicopter at altitude requires a greater angle of attack because of the reduced air density. In forward flight, the situation becomes the same as for an increase in all-up weight.

Also in the hover, the attitude of the fuselage is determined by the position of the CG. The further aft it is, the more tail-down the attitude, which will require a greater forward movement of the cyclic stick to keep the helicopter stationary. Consequently, less cyclic stick is available for forward flight. The situation is reversed when the CG is too far forward.

Characteristics of Blade Stall

Retreating blade stall can be experienced as a result of high forward speed, flying in turbulence, making abrupt or excessive control movements and carrying out manoeuvres with high G loading. The approach of retreating blade stall can be detected by main rotor roughness, erratic stick forces and stick shake. If these conditions are ignored, a pitch-up tendency will develop, followed by a roll toward the retreating side of the rotor disc.

Recovery is achieved by reducing forward speed, reducing collective pitch or reducing the severity of the manoeuvre, or by combining these actions.

Inflow Roll

As previously stated, the effect of air moving horizontally across the rotor disc will reduce the induced flow. This reduction is not uniform, however, because air passing across the disc is continually pulled down by the action of the rotor blades. This means that air moving horizontally toward the disc will cause the greatest reduction in induced flow at the front of the disc, and the smallest reduction at the rear.

This overall reduction in induced flow will cause an increase in rotor thrust, but because the increase in angle of attack is not uniform, the rotor disc will tilt and, combined with the effect of flapback, will roll toward the advancing side.

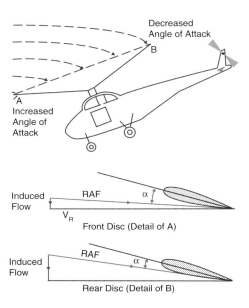

Inflow roll.

Inflow roll will have its greatest effect at low speed, and therefore the axis about which the rotor disc tilts will vary with forward speed. In general, the cyclic stick has to be positioned forward and toward the retreating side to correct these effects in forward flight.

GROUND RESONANCE

Ground resonance can be defined as a vibration of large amplitude resulting from a forced or semi-induced vibration to a mass in contact with, or resting upon, the ground. The helicopter pilot will recognize ground resonance from a rocking motion of the fuselage. If early corrective action is not taken, the amplitude can increase to a point where it becomes uncontrollable and the helicopter will roll over.

Cause of Ground Resonance

If an object is vibrating at its natural frequency, it will continue or damp out depending on the source of the vibration. If a second vibration of the same frequency is present, it will amplify the original vibration, and then the object can resonate to destruction.

Therefore, two vibrations are necessary for resonance to occur.

The initial vibration that causes ground resonance can already be present in the rotor head before the helicopter comes into contact with the ground. Ideally, the rotor disc should have its CG over the centre of rotation, but if its position is displaced for any reason, a 'wobble' will develop. This would have an effect similar to an unbalanced flywheel rotating at speed.

Ground resonance can also be induced if the undercarriage is in light contact with the ground, particularly if the frequency of oscillation of the oleos (dampers) or tyres is in sympathy with the rotor head vibration.

Rotor Head Vibration

Rotor blades should be correctly balanced at manufacture, but flight in icing conditions can cause them to be out of balance due to an uneven accumulation of ice. Moisture absorption can be another cause of unbalance. Pre-flight inspection should always include a check to see that the rotor blade drain holes are unblocked.

On a three-bladed rotor system, the blades should be equally spaced 120 degrees apart. If a rotor drag damper is sticking, the CG of the rotor disc will be displaced away from the axis of rotation.

A rotor blade that is substantially out of track may set up an unbalanced condition, which will be transmitted through the helicopter. This type of unbalance results in nothing more than a 'rough' helicopter and a vibration in the cyclic stick of one beat per revolution. If enough unbalance exists, it is possible that a combination of factors may be encountered that would result in ground resonance being induced.

Vibrations can also be caused through mishandling (over-controlling) the cyclic stick during landing, operating with incorrect or different oleo/tyre pressures, and taxying or making running take-offs and run-on landings over rough ground.

Recovery Action

If flying rpm are available, *lift off immediately*. (Flying rpm should always be maintained until the landing has been completed.)

If flying rpm are not available or if take-off is not practicable, *land immediately*, lowering the collective lever fully, reducing power, applying the brakes and switching off.

VORTEX RING

Although vortices are always present around the edge of the rotor disc, under certain airflow conditions, they will intensify and, coupled with a stall spreading outward from the blade root, result in a sudden loss of rotor thrust and a subsequent rapid loss of height. In some ways, this condition is similar to stalling in a fixed-wing aeroplane. When it occurs, the helicopter is said to be in a state of *vortex ring* (in the USA, often called settling with power).

Causes

This condition can be entered from more than one manoeuvre, but the airflow conditions that cause it remain the same. Vortex ring can only occur when *all* of the following are present:

- Power on (giving an induced flow down through the rotor disc).
- High rate of descent (producing an external airflow directly opposing the induced flow).
- Low forward speed.

Development

When the helicopter is hovering in still-air conditions, the direction of the relative airflow can be determined from the rotor blades' rotational velocity and the induced flow, both of which will have their greatest value near the tip of the blade, but because of blade washout, the root end will have the greatest angle of attack.

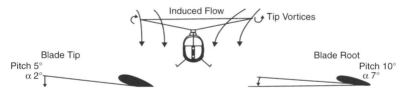

Development of vortex ring.

Consider the effect of lowering the collective pitch lever to begin a descent. When the descent is established, a new airflow component will exist, directly opposing the induced flow, which in turn will alter the direction of the relative airflow along the rotor blade.

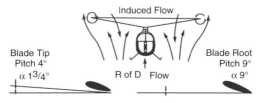

Opposing airflows.

At the blade root, the airflow from the rate of descent will oppose the induced flow, thereby increasing the angle of attack. In the area of the blade tip, the upward flow of air will join and intensify the tip vortices, increase the induced flow and reduce the angle of attack.

If the collective pitch lever is lowered further, the rate of descent will increase, and the process will be repeated until eventually a condition will be attained where the root end of the rotor blade reaches its stalling angle. At this stage, rotor thrust will be decreasing at the blade tip due to the vortices, and at the blade root because of the stalled condition, leaving an area in between to produce the necessary rotor thrust to balance weight.

Blade stall.

Any further lowering of the collective pitch lever will result in a higher rate of descent, which will reduce the area of the blade that is effectively producing rotor thrust; once a condition is reached where rotor thrust becomes insufficient to balance weight, the rate of descent will increase rapidly.

Wind-tunnel experiments have shown that tip vortices form and intensify in a most erratic manner. Dissymmetry of rotor thrust occurs and the helicopter will pitch, roll and yaw to no set pattern, making control extremely difficult.

In the fully developed vortex ring state, raising the collective pitch lever will only aggravate the condition. Instead of reducing the rate of descent, actually it will cause it to increase.

The higher the all-up weight of the helicopter, the higher will be the collective pitch setting to maintain height. Consequently, the vortex ring state can occur at an earlier stage if the helicopter is operating at a higher all-up weight than when it is lightly laden.

Symptoms
There are three symptoms of the vortex ring condition:

- Judder and cyclic stick shake.
- Random yawing, rolling and pitching.
- Rapid increase in rate of descent.

Recovery Action

To recover from a state of vortex ring, it is necessary to change the airflow conditions that cause it. The recommended technique is to apply forward cyclic stick to change the disc attitude and gain a higher forward speed so that the rate of descent flow no longer opposes the induced flow. Then wait until there is a positive increase in indicated airspeed before applying power.

Another method is to enter autorotation, but the resulting considerable loss of height by the time a full recovery can be made must be taken into account.

Therefore, the helicopter pilot should avoid the situations likely to cause vortex ring by restricting the rate of descent when airspeed is low. The most likely flight conditions where this will occur will usually be within 500 ft of the ground, when recovery techniques are unlikely to be successful.

AUTOROTATION

Under normal flight conditions, the main rotor drag is overcome with engine power. When an engine malfunctions or is deliberately disengaged from the rotor system, some other force must be used to maintain rotor rpm. This is achieved by lowering the collective pitch lever fully and allowing the helicopter to descend so that the relative airflow approaches the rotor blades in such a manner that the airflow itself provides the driving force. When the helicopter is descending in this manner, it is said to be in a state of *autorotation*.

Although most autorotations are carried out with some forward speed, the reason why the blades continue to turn can best be explained if the helicopter is considered to be autorotating vertically in still air. Under these conditions, if the various forces involved are calculated for one rotor blade, they will be valid for all the other blades, irrespective of their positions during their 360 degrees of travel.

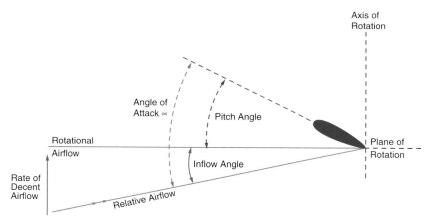

Autorotation angles and inflows.

The various angles and inflows are shown in below. It can be seen that the inflow angle has been determined from the rotor blade's rotational velocity and the airflow caused by the rate of descent.

Autorative Force/Rotor Drag

If we consider three sections of a rotor blade, A, B and C, the direction of the relative airflow for each section can be determined from the blade's rpm and the helicopter's rate of descent. The latter will have a common value for each section, but the rotational velocity will decrease from the tip of the blade toward the root. Therefore, the inflow angle will increase progressively.

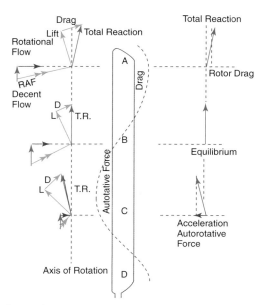

Autorotative force/rotor drag.

Because of the washout incorporated in the rotor blade design, the pitch angle will also increase. Since the blade's angle of attack is the sum of the pitch angle and the inflow angle, the blade's maximum angle of attack will be at the root. If the angle of attack for each section of the blade is known, then by referring to aerofoil data tables, the position of the *total reaction* can be determined, and the vectors of rotor thrust and rotor drag located.

At section A, the condition is the same as for powered flight. The component of total reaction in the plane of rotation *opposes* rotation and will try continually to slow the blade down.

At section B, no part of the total reaction is acting in the plane of rotation – it is all rotor thrust.

At section C, the component of total reaction is in the plane of rotation and *assists* rotation. It will try continually to accelerate the rotor blade. Under these conditions, it is no longer referred to as rotor drag, but is known as the *autorotative force*.

If we now consider the rotor blade as a whole, the section producing an autorotative force will be accelerating the blade, while the section producing rotor drag will be trying to slow it down. To maintain a constant rotor rpm, the autorotative section must be capable of balancing the rotor drag section of the blade plus any ancillary drag (drive shafts, gears, tail rotor, etc.).

Under normal conditions, with the collective lever fully lowered, the autorotative rpm should remain in the correct operating band, provided an adequate rate of descent exists. If the collective pitch lever is raised during autorotation, the pitch angles will increase on all sections of the rotor blade, causing the autorotative section to move outward. At the same time, section D at the root will stall; the extra drag generated will cause a reduction in the size of the autorotative section and an rpm decrease.

Autorotation from high altitudes and/or high all-up weights produces higher rates of descent. Inflow angles will be higher, and the autorotative sections further outboard along the rotor blades. Therefore, rpm will be higher.

Autorotation in Forward Flight

The autorotative force in forward flight is produced in exactly the same way as when the helicopter is in a vertical descent in still air. Because of the changing inflow angle that occurs across the disc in forward flight, however, the autorotative section for the disc as a whole will move toward the retreating side, where the angle of attack is greater.

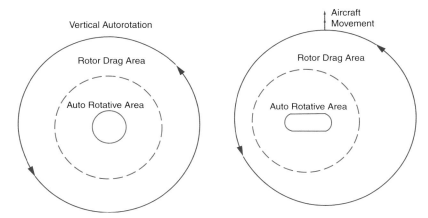

Autorotative area of rotor disc.

If the engine fails during a hover in still air and the pilot lowers the collective pitch lever fully, the helicopter will accelerate downward until such time as the angle of attack produces a total reaction to give an autorotative force to maintain rotor rpm, and a rotor thrust to equal weight. When this condition has been established, the acceleration will stop and the helicopter will continue at a steady rate of descent. If some outside influence causes the angle of attack to increase, there will be an automatic reduction in the rate of descent, the reverse occurring if the angle of attack is decreased.

Compared with a vertical autorotation in still air, initially the rate of descent will decrease with forward speed, but beyond a certain speed, the rate of descent will start to increase again. The reason for this variation of rate of descent with forward speed is the changing direction of the relative airflow.

Relative Airflow – Vertical Autorotation
Consider a helicopter of a given weight, which requires a mean angle of attack of 8 degrees to provide the required rotor thrust and autorotative forces to keep it in a vertical autorotation, and that this angle of attack is obtained when the rate of descent is 2,000 ft/min. If the inflow angle is determined from the rate of descent and a mean rotational velocity, it will be found to have a value of, say 10 degrees.

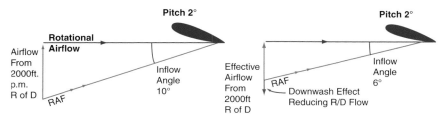

Relative airflow – vertical autorotation.

Because the action of the blades slows down the airflow coming from below the disc, however, the *actual* inflow angle will be less, say 6 degrees. If the mean pitch value of the blade is 2 degrees, the angle of attack will be 8 degrees, the angle required. So 2,000 ft/min rate of descent is required by this helicopter to produce an inflow angle of 6 degrees.

Relative Airflow – Forward Speed
In determining the direction of the relative airflow when the helicopter is in a forward autorotation, three factors must be taken into account. The effect of these factors on the inflow angle will be considered first individually, and then collectively.

Individual Effect
Factor A To achieve forward autorotation, the disc must be tilted forward. Assuming the effective airflow from the rate of descent remains unchanged, the inflow angle must decrease. Therefore, the angle of attack will decrease, as will the rotor thrust. This will cause an increase in rate of descent.

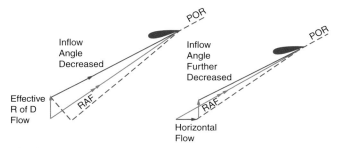

Decrease of inflow angle.

Factor B When the helicopter is moving forward, in addition to the rate of descent flow, the disc will also be subjected to a horizontal airflow. Because the disc is tilted to this horizontal airflow, it will *reduce* the inflow angle. The angle of attack will be decreased, causing an increase to the rate of descent.

Factor C When the helicopter moves forward, the disc will be moving into air that has not been slowed down by the action of the rotor's downwash to the same extent as when the helicopter is descending vertically. Therefore, the *effective* rate of descent airflow will increase, resulting in the inflow angle increasing. The angle of attack and rotor thrust will increase, giving a decreased rate of descent.

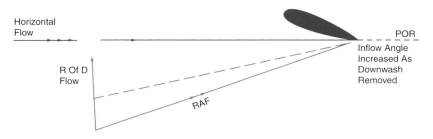

Increase of inflow angle.

Combined Effect
Only a small amount of disc tilt is required for low forward speed. The effect of factor C is greater than the effects of factors A and B combined. The inflow angle increases, angle of attack increases, rotor thrust increases and rate of descent decreases.

The inflow angle reduces as the rate of descent reduces. Stabilization in the rate of descent occurs when the angle of attack is such that rotor thrust equals weight.

Factor C will increase the inflow angle as forward speed increases. As with induced flow in normal powered flight, however, while this increase is large initially, it will reduce as forward speed increases.

As forward speed increases so does parasite drag and the tilt of the rotor to provide the speed increase. Factors A and B quickly increase, and there comes a point where their combined effects equal factor C, when balance is achieved. When this occurs, the helicopter will be flying at a speed that gives the minimum rate of descent. Beyond this speed, the effects of factors A and B will be greater than factor C, and imbalance occurs. Inflow angle and rotor thrust will reduce. To achieve balance again, the required rotor thrust can only be obtained from a higher rate of descent.

Rate of Descent Requirements in Autorotation

In autorotation, components of rate of descent will be required to:

- Produce a rotor thrust equal to weight.
- Provide an autorotative force to maintain the selected rotor rpm.
- Produce a thrust component equal to parasite drag.

If these three components are plotted against forward speed, the graph would be similar to the one showing the power requirements for level flight.

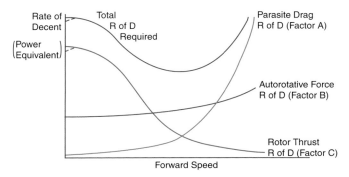

Rate of descent requirements in autorotation.

Autorating for Endurance and Range in Still Air

Endurance means autorotating to stay in the air as long as possible. This must be done at a speed that gives the minimum rate of descent. Therefore, the speed for endurance will correspond to the lowest part on the 'rate of descent' curve.

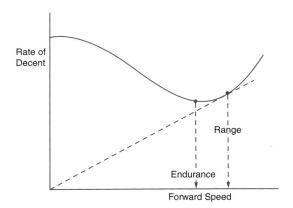

Autorotating for endurance and range.

Maximum range will be achieved when the helicopter is descending along its shallowest flight path. This is achieved when flying at the best forward speed/rate of descent ratio. On the graph, the optimum ratio will be at the speed where a line drawn from the graph point of origin is tangential to the 'rate of descent' curve.

Range and endurance information, including rotor rpm settings, is normally quoted in the flight manual for the helicopter type.

Flare

The flare effect in autorotation will be exactly the same as for a flare in powered flight. Rotor rpm will rise because the increased inflow angle will cause the autorotative section of the rotor blade to move further out toward the blade tip. The increased rotor thrust will reduce the rate of descent while the flare lasts.

Autorotative Landing

When engine failure occurs in flight, the helicopter has potential energy to dissipate. This is converted into kinetic energy during the autorotative descent.

When close to the ground, the kinetic energy stored in the rotor system by virtue of its rpm is converted into work in the form of a large increase in rotor thrust by use of the collective pitch lever. Thus, the landing is cushioned, but the rotor rpm decay rapidly as the kinetic energy is used up.

Avoid Area

All helicopter manuals contain an Avoid Area graph drawn for the particular type of helicopter. The shaded areas indicate the height/airspeed zones where, in the event of a power failure, either a full autorotation may not be possible before reaching the ground, or forward speed cannot be reduced sufficiently for a safe landing to be carried out. Continuous operation in these areas should be avoided unless it is operationally necessary.

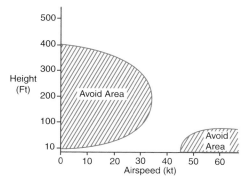

Avoid area for autorotations.

FLYING FOR RANGE AND ENDURANCE

Definitions

Range The *distance* in air nautical miles that can be covered for a given quantity of fuel.

Endurance The period of *time* that an aircraft can remain airborne for a given quantity of fuel.

For both range and endurance, the criterion is fuel consumption. The pilot must achieve the minimum fuel consumption in straight and level flight for endurance flying, and maximum efficiency for range flying; in other words, the best ratio of *distance* covered to *fuel consumed*.

Endurance Flying – Piston-Engined Helicopters

In a piston-engined helicopter, fuel consumption is proportional to the power produced. Therefore, the power required for level flight conditions can also be said to represent the fuel consumption for the same conditions.

In the Power Required vs Airspeed graph below, it can be seen that minimum power is required at a particular airspeed if altitude and all-up weight are constant (point A). It follows, therefore, that at this speed, there is a minimum fuel consumption, thus satisfying endurance requirements.

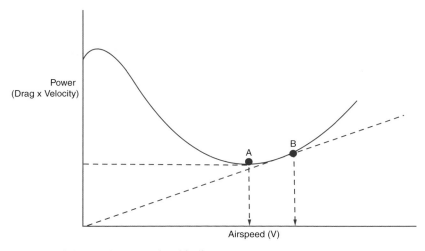

Endurance flying – piston-engined helicopters.

Range Flying – Piston-Engined Helicopters

When a given quantity of fuel is consumed, a certain amount of work can be produced:

Fuel consumed = Work done = Force × Distance

(The force overcome aerodynamically is drag)

Therefore, Work done = Drag × Distance

$$\text{Now, Power} = \frac{\text{Workdone}}{\text{Time}} = \frac{\text{Drag} \times \text{Distance}}{\text{Time}} = \text{Drag} \times \text{Velocity}$$

Referring to the power graph again, the vertical must represent Drag × Velocity, and the base line Velocity, or True Airspeed (TAS).

If a line is drawn from the graph origin to the power curve, the lowest angle (point B) gives the airspeed for *minimum drag* and corresponds to the range speed.

Turbine Helicopters

The fuel consumption of a turbine engine is proportional to the *thrust* being produced. At a steady speed, thrust equals drag. Therefore, if we consider the speed where there is minimum drag, there must also be minimum thrust and, hence, minimum fuel consumption. This is known as *endurance speed*.

The turbine-engined helicopter does not provide pure thrust, but converts it into *torque* (shaft horsepower) to drive the rotor shaft. Therefore, it is similar to a compromise between piston and turbine engines. Consequently, the endurance speed for a turbine helicopter is between the minimum-power speed and the minimum-drag speed.

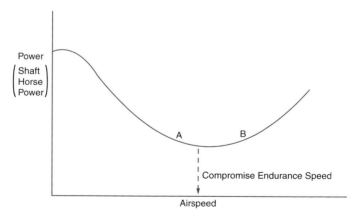

Endurance flying – turbine helicopters.

To achieve maximum range with a turbine helicopter, it is necessary to obtain maximum efficiency from both the engine and the airframe. The airframe is most efficient at minimum-drag speed. Engine efficiency improves with high engine rpm, a lower specific fuel consumption usually being achieved at a speed greater than the minimum-drag speed. Therefore, a compromise is necessary for maximum range. The best compromise is to be found at the best TAS/drag ratio, which occurs when a tangent is drawn to the 'drag' curve.

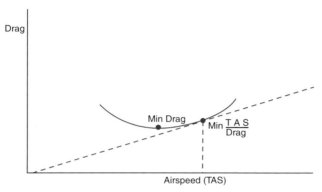

Maximum range compromise.

Engine Efficiency at Altitude

The turbocharged piston engine improves with an increase in altitude until the throttle butterfly valve is fully open for a given manifold pressure setting (*full-throttle height*). Thereafter, efficiency and power decrease.

The efficiency of the turbine engine improves as altitude increases, because thermal efficiency improves (air is colder) and the compressor load decreases with reduced air density. Thus, engine rpm increase, and specific fuel consumption improves.

Wind Velocity

Because of the relatively low speed range of the helicopter, wind can and does have a large effect on range flying. In fact, it can be the main factor to consider when selecting the best height at which to fly. Choosing a higher altitude may give an advantage of a strong tail wind; conversely, a strong head wind may make it better to fly low to improve ground speed and distance.

WEIGHT AND BALANCE

Definitions

Basic Weight The weight of the helicopter, including its basic equipment, full oil and unusable fuel, to which it is only necessary to add the weights of variable, expendable and payload items.

Basic Equipment The non-expendable equipment that is common to all the roles for which the helicopter is designed. It includes unusable fluids, coolant, and hydraulic and pneumatic systems.

Variable Load Items that vary from flight to flight, which are not expendable in the air, such as crew and role equipment.

Expendable Load Includes fuel, oil and freight that may be air dropped.

Payload The total load of passengers and/or freight actually carried in the helicopter.

Maximum All-Up Weight The maximum weight at which the helicopter is permitted to fly.

Balance

Having determined that the helicopter will not exceed the limitations of all-up weight, the load must be positioned correctly to ensure that the CG remains within limits.

When hovering in still-air conditions, the attitude of the fuselage will vary with the position of the CG, and it may be necessary to apply cyclic stick to keep the rotor disc level. Provided that the CG remains within specified limits, cyclic stick will be adequate for forward and rearward flight.

The lateral CG position normally changes very little with internal and external loads. Any lateral displacement requires a compensating cyclic stick movement if the rotor disc is to remain level. To avoid running out of cyclic stick control, it is important not to exceed any lateral limitations.

Determining the Centre of Gravity

The CG position is determined by finding the moment of individual items of equipment about a given datum, adding together all the moments and then dividing that total by the total weight.

The turning moment is found by multiplying the weight of an object by its distance from the datum. Provided that all the moments are taken about the same datum, it is immaterial where the datum lies. (*See The Helicopter Pilot's Manual, Volume 2* for a more in-depth explanation of weight and balance.)

It is important to note that with some helicopters, there is a large change in the CG position as a result of fuel consumption. Consequently, although the helicopter may be within the CG limits for take-off, it can go beyond the limits during flight.

STABILITY

When a helicopter is disturbed from its flight path and tries to return to that state without any input from the pilot, it is said to be *stable*. Stability is best explained as static stability and dynamic stability.

Static Stability

If an object is disturbed, but returns to its original position by its own accord, it is said to be *statically stable*.

If, after being disturbed, the object continues to move further away, it is said to be *statically unstable*.

If, after being disturbed, the object assumes a position that is different from the original, it is said to be *statically neutrally stable*.

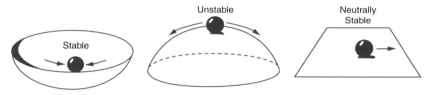

Static stability.

Dynamic Stability

If an object is statically stable, it will return to its original position, but in doing so, it may overshoot the position initially. If the amplitude of the oscillations dies out, it is said to be *dynamically stable*.

If the amplitude of the oscillations increases, it is said to be *dynamically unstable*.

If the oscillations continue, but at a constant amplitude, it is said to be *dynamically neutrally stable*.

Stability in the Hover

Imagine a helicopter hovering in still air when a gust of wind develops from the side. The rotor disc will flap away from the gust, and if no corrective action is taken, the helicopter will move downwind.

After a short while, the gust dies out, but because the helicopter is moving sideways, it will experience an airflow coming from the opposite direction. The rotor disc will flap away from this new airflow, slowing the helicopter. In addition, the fuselage will tend to 'follow through' and cause the rotor disc to be tilted even further so that the helicopter moves back toward its original position faster than it moved away.

This movement will result in the helicopter experiencing continual sideways changes in airflow affecting the rotor disc, and although it will be statically stable, because the amplitude of the oscillations will be continually increasing, it will be dynamically unstable.

The same effect will be produced no matter what the direction of the gust. Therefore, the helicopter is dynamically unstable in the pitching and rolling planes.

Stability in Forward Flight

If a gust of wind hits the rotor disc from ahead in forward flight, it will cause the disc to tilt back, thereby reducing forward thrust. The helicopter will decelerate, but as it does so, the inertia of the fuselage will cause it to pitch up, tilting the rotor disc even more to slow the helicopter more rapidly.

When the speed has stabilized, the fuselage will start to pitch down below its original position because of a pendulum effect (pendulosity), while at the same time, the rotor disc will flap forward relative to the fuselage (reduced flapback effect due to lower speed). This results in a speed increase with the helicopter in a shallow descent. As the speed increases, the rotor disc will begin to experience flapback again, and the whole cycle will be repeated, but with increasing amplitude. If no cyclic stick correction is applied, the helicopter could end up pitching outside its control limits.

Therefore, the helicopter is statically stable, because each oscillation will take it through its original position, but is dynamically unstable because the amplitude of the oscillations increases progressively.

If a gust of wind strikes from the right side, and the tail rotor is mounted on the left side, the immediate effect is for the tail rotor's angle of attack to decrease and the helicopter to yaw to the right. However, the inertia of the helicopter will continue to keep it on its original flight path. Then weathercock action will return the fuselage to its original position.

From this, we can say that in the *yawing plane*, the helicopter is both statically and dynamically stable.

Pendulosity

The limit of control in a helicopter is determined by the amount by which it is possible to tilt the rotor disc, as this determines the tilt of the rotor thrust line. For a condition of equilibrium to exist, the CG must align itself with the total rotor thrust line. The greater the distance between the main rotor head (centre of thrust line) and the position of the CG, the more the attitude of the helicopter can change before reaching control limits.

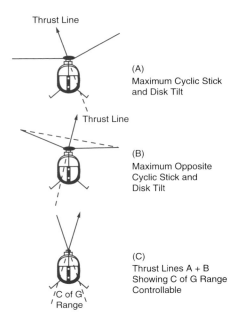

Thrust Line

(A)
Maximum Cyclic Stick
and Disk Tilt

Thrust Line

(B)
Maximum Opposite
Cyclic Stick and
Disk Tilt

(C)
Thrust Lines A + B
Showing C of G Range
Controllable

C of G
Range

Pendulosity.

Stability Aids

One method of improving stability in forward flight is to fit a *horizontal stabilizer* to the rear of the fuselage. This will help to prevent the fuselage from 'following through' when a gust of wind causes flapback. As the fuselage begins to pitch up, the increasing angle of attack on the stabilizer will damp down the movement, thereby reducing the rearward tilt of the rotor disc. The reverse occurs when the fuselage tilts down.

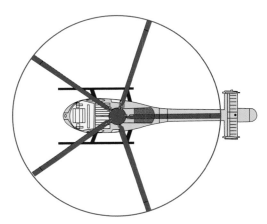

Horizontal stabilizer.

69

Adverse effects from the stabilizer can be produced when the helicopter is moving backward. If a gust of wind causes the rotor disc to flap forward, the fuselage will slow down and the tail will pitch up, increasing the angle of attack on the stabilizer and causing the tail to pitch up even more.

Not all helicopters have horizontal stabilizers.

Control Power

This can be defined as the effectiveness of the cyclic stick in achieving changes in fuselage attitude. The main factor determining the degree of control power is the distance from the main rotor shaft at which the cyclic stick force is effective. This, in turn, is dependent on the type of rotor system employed on the helicopter.

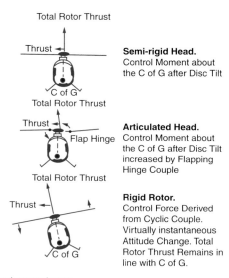

Control power and rotor systems.

Semi-Rigid System

If a cyclic pitch change is made on a semi-rigid rotor head, the rotor disc plane alters and the total rotor thrust acting through the main rotor shaft is tilted. This produces a moment about the CG position, and an attitude change occurs.

Fully Articulated System

Again, a cyclic pitch change alters the plane of the main rotor disc and tilts the total rotor thrust, but the point at which cyclic force acts in effecting a fuselage attitude change is not only the main shaft. The plus and minus application of cyclic pitch, as well as changing the main rotor disc plane, is also felt at the flapping hinges. Thus, a couple is formed that is additional to the single force of the total rotor thrust in the semi-rigid head and, therefore, is more effective.

Rigid System

A cyclic pitch change sets up an immediate aerodynamic couple to alter the fuselage attitude. The couple is estimated to be the equivalent of placing flapping hinges on an articulated rotor head at 17 per cent rotor radius from the shaft. If the same cyclic force were applied to the three rotor systems, the rigid rotor would be the most effective in changing the helicopter's attitude. The articulated rotor would be the next best, and the semi-rigid rotor the least effective in terms of control power.

TYPICAL EXAMINATION QUESTIONS

1. During steady forward flight, the forces acting on the helicopter are:
   a) lift, equal and opposite to weight; horizontal thrust opposite to, but greater than, drag.
   b) lift, equal and opposite to weight; horizontal thrust, equal and opposite to drag.
   c) lift, opposite to, but greater than, weight; horizontal thrust, equal and opposite to drag.

2. Rise and fall of a main rotor blade from a mean position during rotor rotation is called:
   a) resonance.
   b) flapping.
   c) phase lead lag.

3. The angle between the main rotor blade longitudinal axis and the tip-path plane is the:
   a) coning angle.
   b) angle of attack.
   c) blade pitch angle.

4. Cyclic stick movement:
   a) changes the coning angle.
   b) alters the disc attitude.
   c) changes the advance angle.

5. To increase total rotor thrust, the helicopter pilot must:
   a) decrease the angle of attack of the main rotor blades via a collective pitch control.
   b) increase the angle of attack of the rotor blades via the cyclic stick.
   c) increase the angle of attack of the rotor blades via the collective pitch control.

6. The total rotor thrust derived from the main rotor is largely due to:
   a) the centrifugal effects of the rotating blades.
   b) aerofoil blade sections creating a low-pressure region on their upper surfaces.
   c) aerofoil blade sections creating a high-pressure region on their upper surfaces.

7. A vortex ring state of the main rotor blades:
   a) is a vortex creating a stalled condition at the root end, caused by high forward speed.
   b) refers to the tip vortices that occur in normal flight.
   c) causes an even higher rate of descent when descending with power on.

8. During one revolution of the main rotor blades, blade flap is the:

   a) rise and fall of the blades due to varying angular velocity.
   b) angular movement in the horizontal plane due to varying angular velocity.
   c) rise and fall of the blades due to varying aerodynamic lift.

9. The design maximum forward speed of a helicopter is either governed by the speed of the advancing blade approaching the speed of sound or by:

   a) the retreating blade approaching the stalled condition.
   b) the advancing blade approaching the stalled condition.
   c) the amount of collective pitch increase available.

10. One secondary effect that the tail rotor tends to produce, if not corrected, is sideways drift:

   a) in the opposite direction to the tail rotor thrust caused by the main rotor torque reaction.
   b) in the direction of tail rotor thrust.
   c) in either direction depending on the amount of tail rotor thrust applied.

11. An increase in rotor rpm causes:

   a) decreased centripetal acceleration.
   b) increased centrifugal force.
   c) increased coning angle.

12. When hovering near the ground:

   a) lift is lost due to the increase in pressure under the rotor.
   b) extra lift is obtained because of the increase in pressure under the rotor.
   c) extra lift is obtained because of the decrease in pressure under the rotor.

13. Phase lag is the:

   a) time between collective pitch increase and the restoration of the original rotor rpm.
   b) time between cyclic control inputs and rotor disc attitude change.
   c) angle through which a blade moves between a pitch selection and the corresponding flapped position.

14. During autorotative descent, main rotor rpm are maintained by:

   a) a lift force component created by the upflow of air.
   b) form drag acting as torque after the reversal of airflow to upward.
   c) the inertia of the rotor head and blades.

15. Dynamic roll-over may be caused by:

   a) excessive yaw pedal movements to either the left or right.

    b) an excessive rolling moment developing about a skid or wheel in contact with a slope or uneven ground.

    c) excessive movement of the cyclic stick in pitch only.

16. The purpose of fitting a horizontal stabilizer to a helicopter is:

    a) to counteract some of the nose-down tendency in level flight.

    b) the primary method of pitch attitude control.

    c) to compensate for CG movement in flight.

17. When rotating, the main rotor blade, being of aerofoil section, derives lift:

    a) by producing a high-pressure area above the blade.

    b) by producing a low-pressure area above the blade.

    c) by acting like a screw on the air, allowing for slippage.

18. Stalling of a main rotor blade may occur on the:

    a) retreating blade at high forward speed.

    b) advancing blade at high forward speed.

    c) retreating blade at low forward speed.

19. The drag force of a rotor blade is opposed by:

    a) rotor rpm.

    b) blade flapping.

    c) torque.

20. Changes in magnitude of total rotor thrust from the main rotor during cruise are achieved by:

    a) varying the speed of the main rotor while the pitch of the blade is substantially constant.

    b) combined rotor speed change and blade pitch change.

    c) altering the pitch of the main rotor blades collectively while the rotor speed is kept substantially constant.

21. Ground resonance is:

    a) a standing wave vibration set up between the main rotor and the ground.

    b) a sympathetic vibration caused by main rotor and landing gear interaction.

    c) an effect that amplifies engine and/or tail rotor vibration on the ground.

22. The pitch angle of a main rotor blade at its most forward position is affected by:

    a) fore and aft cyclic stick movement.

    b) left and right cyclic stick movement.

    c) forward cyclic stick movement only.

23. Turning the helicopter in hovering flight may be achieved by the pedals changing the:
    a) cyclic pitch of the tail rotor.
    b) speed of the tail rotor.
    c) collective pitch of the tail rotor blades.

24. When the collective pitch lever is raised, the angle of attack:
    a) of all the main rotor blades is decreased equally.
    b) of all the main rotor blades is increased equally.
    c) of the blade in the forward position is increased while the angle of attack of the blade in the aft position is decreased.

25. Disc loading is defined as:
    a) an increase in rotor thrust required to compensate for accelerations during manoeuvres.
    b) maximum centrifugal loading of the rotor hub assembly.
    c) the ratio of the total weight of the helicopter supported per unit of disc area.

Answers

1. b	10. b	18. a
2. b	11. b	19. c
3. a	12. b	20. c
4. b	13. c	21. b
5. c	14. a	22. b
6. b	15. b	23. c
7. c	16. a	24. b
8. c	17. b	25. c
9. a		

2 GENERAL HANDLING

SAFETY AROUND HELICOPTERS

Helicopters are very safe flying machines as long as they are operated within the parameters established by the manufacturer. There are certain basic aspects of helicopter operation, however, that require special consideration to ensure safety.

Rotors and Immovable Objects

The exposed nature of the main and tail rotors deserves special caution. Care must be taken when hover taxiing near hangars or obstructions, since the distance between the rotor blade tips and the obstruction can be very difficult to judge.

The tail rotor of many helicopters cannot be seen from the cabin. Therefore, when hovering backward or turning on a spot, plenty of room must be allowed for tail rotor clearance.

Allow tail rotor clearance.

Rotors and People

People are fascinated by helicopters, so caution must be used when operating close to the public. If people are to be allowed to approach a helicopter or just to be near it, they should have been instructed in the safe techniques to use beforehand.

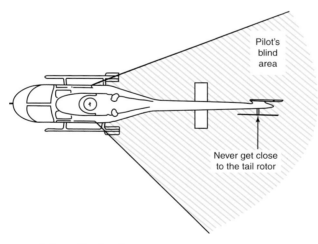

Always approach from the front.

A helicopter should always be approached or departed from the front. People approaching the helicopter when the blades are turning should be instructed to stay low as they pass under the rotor disc. Gusts of wind can cause the rotor blades to flex low enough for the tips to hit a person of average height. They should also be instructed to hold on firmly to any hats or loose articles and *never* to reach up or chase after an object that has been blown away from them.

Approach and Leave the
Helicopter in a Crouched Manner.

Hold on to your hat.

Duck low when approaching or leaving the helicopter.

Loose items can be drawn up into the main rotor.

People should *never* be permitted to move to the rear of the cabin doors, thereby disappearing from the pilot's view. Ducking under the tail boom should be *absolutely forbidden* due to the close proximity of the tail rotor.

Consideration should also be given to the slope of the ground around the helicopter. Always *approach up* the slope, and *leave down* the slope, because the main rotor blade tips are closer to the ground on the up-slope side.

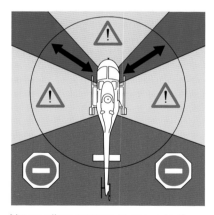

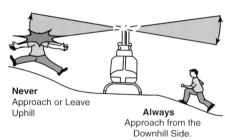

Never
Approach or Leave
Uphill

Always
Approach from the
Downhill Side.

Never allow anyone to move to the rear of the cabin doors.

Approach upslope; leave downslope.

Rotors and Debris

Another consideration is the downwash that the main rotors generate. This is capable of blowing sand, dust, snow and water at very high velocity for quite significant distances. This flying debris can cause injury to nearby people, and may even damage buildings or other aircraft.

In addition, any airborne debris near the helicopter can be ingested into the engine intake or struck by the main and tail rotor blades.

Rotors and RPM

Rotor rpm is a very important aspect of helicopter performance. The normal operating range is limited to the green region marked on the face of the rotor tachometer.

Rotor rpm gauge.

Minimum Rotor Speed

Several aspects of performance are incorporated into the minimum rotor speed. First, tail rotor speed is a function of main rotor speed. At low main rotor rpm, the tail rotor may not be able to produce enough thrust to counteract main rotor torque. In this case, directional control may be inadequate to prevent the helicopter from rotating.

Rotor speed also relates to the thrust, or lift, produced. As the main rotor speed decreases, thrust is reduced by a factor of approximately two; that is, a decrease in rpm of 10 per cent results in a decrease in lift of almost 20 per cent. A main rotor speed below the minimum limit will not produce enough thrust to sustain level flight.

One of the most important criteria associated with minimum rotor speed is autorotation performance. Helicopters must have the capability to autorotate to a safe landing to be certified. The minimum rotor rpm provides adequate controllability during an autorotative descent and landing. Below the minimum rotor rpm, this capability is questionable.

Maximum Rotor Speed

The maximum rotor speed is a structural consideration. The rotor blades, main rotor head and transmission have additional load factors incorporated into their designs. The integrity of the rotor is protected by not exceeding the maximum permitted rotor speed.

Airspeed Considerations

Helicopters are highly manoeuvrable flying machines. As such, they can be flown at 3 ft or 300 ft above the ground at speeds ranging from a standstill to the maximum specified by the manufacturer.

Certain airspeed and altitude combinations must be avoided, however, to provide favourable autorotation performance in the event of an engine failure. Likewise, the maximum speed of a helicopter is limited by aerodynamic considerations. These aspects of performance must be considered in all helicopter operations.

THE HEIGHT/VELOCITY DIAGRAM

All manufacturers publish a height/velocity (avoid curve) diagram in the heliopter's flight manual. The diagram depicts unsafe combinations of altitude and airspeed. Operating at heights and speeds within the marked areas will not allow enough time to establish safe autorotation in the event of an engine failure.

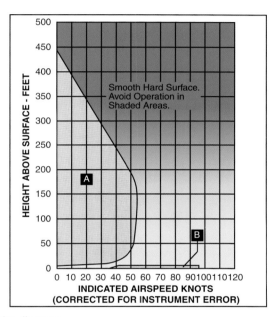

Height/velocity diagram.

Since the diagram is drawn for flight at constant speed and height, an engine failure during climb out is much more critical. During the climb, the helicopter is operating at higher power settings and rotor blade pitch angles. Therefore, an engine failure at this time would cause rapid decay of rotor rpm.

Avoid conditions of low height and high airspeed, because your recognition of an engine failure will probably coincide with, or occur shortly after, ground contact! Even if you do detect an engine failure immediately, there may not be sufficient time to rotate the helicopter from a nose-low attitude to one that is suitable for slowing the aircraft down for landing.

As a rule, if the helicopter is more than 500 ft above the ground, you should have sufficient time to establish a steady autorotation. Between approximately 12 ft and 500 ft, the ability to transition into autorotation depends on the actual height and airspeed at the time the engine fails. Below 12 ft, you can make a safe autorotative landing by utilizing the inertia of the main rotor blades. That is why it is important to familiarize yourself with the height/velocity diagram for every helicopter type you fly.

PRE-FLIGHT INSPECTION

Safe Flying Begins on the Ground

A pre-flight inspection is carried out prior to each flight to ensure that the helicopter is in a safe condition. The pilot in command is the person responsible for ensuring that the aircraft is in a safe condition.

Always pre-flight a helicopter with care, especially one that has remained unused for some time. Birds, insects and small animals often choose inactive aircraft as nesting places. Air ducts, pitot tubes and fuel vents are typical areas that could be obstructed by such pests.

Always use a check-list when making a pre-flight inspection.

Regardless of the number of times a procedure is repeated, a printed check-list should be followed step by step each time. A check-list is used because of variations in types of helicopter and is essential for the following reasons:

- It provides an organized procedure for a complex operation.
- It prevents duplication of effort while ensuring each item is checked.
- It ensures that no important item is missed.
- It helps in making the transition to different models of helicopter.
- It eliminates the possibility of forgetting items.

ENVIRONMENTAL FLYING

Excessive aircraft noise can result not only in discomfort and inconvenience to people on the ground, but also in the possibility of mandatory flying restrictions being imposed over certain areas of the countryside. It is particularly undesirable near built-up areas, schools, hospitals, churches and outdoor assemblies of people.

Reaction to helicopter noise will be adverse and strong if the sound is too irritating or represents something that seems to threaten safety.

Although many commercial operators include environmental flying in their Operations Manuals, it is up to all helicopter pilots to fly in such a way as to make the sound of their machine as unintrusive as possible.

Noise Levels

The noise level of a light helicopter – 5,000 lb (2,270 kg) gross weight or less – is a function of the type of engine fitted. Turbine-engined helicopters are quieter than piston-engined machines, and are no louder that surface transportation vehicles. Note that the noise level of a helicopter at a given gross weight covers a certain range. This is true not only for helicopters in general, but also for particular helicopter types. Therefore, you need to know how you can fly your particular helicopter in the lower portion of the range of sound level.

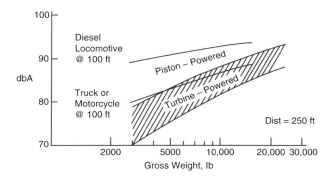

Trend of Helicopter Noise Levels (dbA Units).

Helicopter noise levels.

Source of Helicopter Sound

The acoustical signature of a helicopter is partly due to the modulation of sound by the relatively slow turning main rotor. This modulated sound is often referred to as *blade slap*.

For a typical light helicopter, blade slap occurs during partial power descents, when one rotor blade intersects its own vortex system or that of another blade. When this happens, the rotor blade experiences high velocities and rapid changes in angle of attack. This can drive a section of the rotor blade into compressibility and possibly shock stall, both of which produce variations in aerodynamic loading. Both generate sound.

The figure below indicates where you can expect to produce the most sound in a light helicopter. Maximum blade slap occurs at airspeeds of 65–85 kt (75–98 mph) and rates of descent between 300 and 600 ft/min.

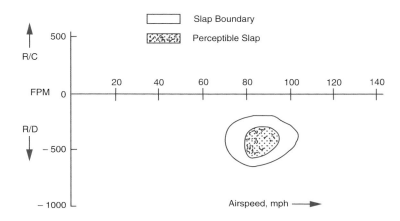

Noisy Flight Operations – Light Helicopters.

Blade slap.

The 'slap boundary' for your particular type of helicopter may be somewhat different to that shown, because the main rotor may slap intermittently when it encounters wind gusts, or if you transition rapidly from one flight condition to another.

Although the sound produced does not seem extremely loud to the pilot, it can be heard and used to define the slap boundaries for your particular helicopter type. Of course, people on the ground hear the noise more readily and notice the blade slap increase in intensity as the helicopter descends.

How to Minimize Noise

In general, you can eliminate the most offensive sounds by flying outside the blade-slap regions for your particular helicopter. When this is not possible, you should fly through them as quickly as you can.

There are other methods of reducing helicopter noise, which you should use whether you are flying in the blade-slap region or not:

Routes and Airspeeds

- Fly at the highest practicable altitude during the approach to built-up areas.
- Select a route into your landing site over the least populated area.

84

- Avoid low flying over residential areas.
- Maintain as high a cruising speed as possible.
- Select your final approach with due regard to the type of area surrounding the landing point.

Noise Abatement Approach and Landing
When beginning final approach, follow one of the following procedures:

- Establish a good rate of descent before reducing airspeed, or hold the rate of descent below 200 ft/min while reducing airspeed to about 60 kt (69 mph), then increase the rate of descent. At a convenient airspeed between 50 and 80 kt (55 and 92 mph), establish the required angle of approach while maintaining a good rate of descent.
- Increase rate of descent if the main rotor tends to slap. Approaching the flare, reduce airspeed to below 60 kt (69 mph) before decreasing rate of descent.

The basic difference between these approach techniques and a normal approach is that they avoid the blade-slap region. Both techniques give approximately the same airspeed during the approach and an approach angle that is a few degrees steeper than the norm.

Once the pilot has transitioned from the cruise and established the approach angle, the airspeed and rate of descent can be adjusted to suit local conditions while operating at minimum noise.

Departure
Transition into the climb out is a reasonably quiet operation. You can limit the total ground area exposed to helicopter noise by using a high rate of climb technique and making a very smooth transition. Your departure route should take you over areas that are the least sensitive to noise.

Meteorological Considerations
Wind has two effects on sound. It carries it in the direction in which it is blowing and it makes a background noise of its own.

In inland areas, surface winds are generally stronger during daytime and weaker at night. In coastal regions, land and sea breezes give a different diurnal pattern. They begin to blow shortly after sunrise (sea breeze) and sunset (land breeze). You can use these winds to increase the acceptability of your helicopter by flying downwind of densely populated areas, and by scheduling the majority of flights near noise-sensitive areas after midday.

Temperature also has two effects on sound. First is the tendency of warm air to be more turbulent than cold air and, therefore, to disperse sound, decreasing its nuisance effect. However, the major effect of temperature depends on the temperature gradient (the change in temperature with altitude). The normal gradient is negative, temperature decreasing with altitude.

Because sound travels faster in warmer air, in an atmosphere with a normal gradient, the lower part of a sound wave tends to outrun the upper part, making propagation, in effect, curve upward and away from the ground.

The negative gradient reaches a maximum in the late morning or just after midday, and is more intense during the summer months. This means that there is some value in scheduling flights to and from noise-sensitive areas during warmer times of the day.

At certain times, however, there may be an inversion in the atmosphere (a layer of air in which the temperature increases with altitude). The inversion reverses the normal curvature of sound propagation, turning an abnormally high proportion of the sound energy back toward the ground.

The most severe inversions usually occur at night and in the early morning. Consequently, these are the times when the sound of the helicopter will have the most adverse effect upon people on the ground. Although environment is hardly a meteorological subject, it is important to mention here that the ground environment has much to do with the intrusiveness of the sound you make with your helicopter.

The background noise level of residential areas is at its lowest point between late evening and early morning. In warm weather, people are apt to be relaxing out of doors in the evenings and at weekends. It is at these times that people are most conscious and resentful of noise intrusion. Therefore, it is at these times that you should be most reluctant to fly noisily.

ICING

Icing presents a very real problem for the helicopter pilot. Despite the ease and rapidity with which a helicopter may usually be landed, there are definite dangers, the avoidance of which calls for alertness and good judgement.

Ice will build up on helicopters in a similar manner, and in similar conditions, to ice accretion on fixed-wing aeroplanes. The outcome, however, may present rather different problems.

Rotors, windshield, fuselage and control linkages may all suffer from icing. During flight in icing conditions, ice may form on all parts of the helicopter simultaneously, or may accumulate on only some parts. It is quite possible for ice to build up on the rotors to a dangerous degree before any is noted on the windshield. Such variations may be explained by the difference in impact velocities and by the differing temperatures created as the air is expanded or compressed by various aerofoil effects.

Rotor Icing

Both main and tail rotors may be affected by icing. Usually, when one rotor suffers from icing, the other will be affected to a similar degree. The main rotor is the more vital of the two, because icing will interfere with lift as well as control capability. The rate of ice build-up on the rotor is dependent on the type of ice encountered.

Ice accretion usually occurs at a slower rate toward the blade tip; however, a covering of a mere $\frac{1}{8}$ in (3 mm) around the leading edges can be sufficient to cause disaster. This high sensitivity to a comparatively thin coating of ice is explained by the fact that the load supported per unit area of the blade surface is extremely high on the outer section of the main rotor disc. This high blade loading may be up to ten times the wing loading of a conventional aeroplane.

Ice accretion on rotor blade.

Critical stages of icing can develop rapidly. During flight, the pilot can get some idea of the degree of ice formation by noting any requirements to increase power that otherwise are unexplained. A wise precaution is to bank the helicopter either way periodically and check the cyclic response. Any discovery of sluggishness should be followed by a landing at the earliest possible opportunity.

The helicopter pilot must be particularly wary of the pitfall of failing to realize early the full significance of the predicament. Under main rotor icing conditions, cruise flight may present little difficulties, but as soon as speed is reduced, there may be insufficient power, or control, to bring the helicopter to the hover.

The most significant point in all of this is that it *can* happen, and happen quickly, before any visual signs appear elsewhere on the helicopter.

Windshield and Fuselage Icing

Ice will normally appear on the windshield and fuselage at the same time. In this situation, the pilot can readily observe the type of ice and rate of build-up. Fortunately, this type of icing will usually form with, or before, the build-up of ice on the critical parts of the main rotor.

Under most conditions, this ice will serve as an adequate warning to the pilot to suspect icing elsewhere. Quite often, ice will form on the fuselage, but not on the rotor blades, except, near the blade roots, which will be moving comparatively slowly. Here, the ice has relatively little aerodynamic effect, but the pilot must remember that ice on the fuselage usually infers that it is forming at much the same rate on the control linkages. For this reason, the pilot should frequently exercise the controls through their full limits to ensure proper response.

The other effects of windshield and fuselage icing are more obvious. The pilot's forward view will become restricted, although this rarely presents a problem. Fuselage icing, of course, has a cumulative weight penalty, which, when added to rotor icing, can be dangerous.

Most light helicopters are prohibited from flight in icing conditions.

DISORIENTATION

The helicopter pilot is far more dependent upon constant, adequate visual references than is his counterpart in a fixed-wing aeroplane. This is because the helicopter is less stable in all directions of movement and will change its attitude far more suddenly than the aeroplane. The reduced acceleration forces and the higher levels of vibration make such changes harder to detect if visual reference is lost momentarily. Furthermore, the sluggish reaction to control corrections by many helicopters prevents recovery at low level if the correction is not initiated at a sufficiently early stage.

A helicopter pilot who has entered cloud inadvertently and can no longer perceive outside references will quickly become unable to tell which way is up. This is because balance organs and nerve endings, for the most part, depend upon a correct orientation to the pull of gravity. The brain struggles to decipher signals being sent from the senses, but without the clues normally supplied by vision (horizon), incorrect or conflicting interpretations may result.

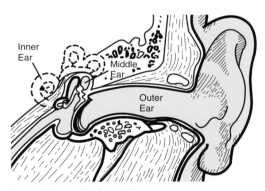

Balance organs depend on pull of gravity.

Vertigo

The outcome of such sensory confusion is a dizzy, whirling sensation called *vertigo* (sometimes called *spacial disorientation*). Vertigo may occur in various forms and may be produced by a number of different flight situations. A pilot on a night flight, for example, flying toward an inclined cloudbank that is well illuminated by moonlight may well experience sensory confusion. This is because most people naturally assume a cloud layer to be parallel to the surface of the earth. Because the cloudbank is inclined, the pilot might attempt to level the helicopter with it, thereby initiating a turn.

Sensory confusion can affect control inputs.

In turbulence, if a helicopter is rolled sharply to the right or left, then slowly resumes straight and level flight, the pilot may be aware of the roll, but not of the recovery. If the helicopter rolls very slowly to the left or right, the pilot might still believe the helicopter to be in straight and level flight. Attitude changes of up to 20 degrees from the horizontal may go unnoticed if made very slowly and without outside visual references.

A common type of sensory confusion occurs when a helicopter pilot, who has not been fully trained in instrument flying, accidentally enters cloud. Often, the helicopter will enter with a very slight bank at a rate undetectable to the senses. Usually, this bank will increase until there is a noticeable loss of altitude. The pilot notes this and, still thinking the helicopter is straight and level, may pull back slightly on the cyclic and apply some power in an attempt to correct the situation. This only serves to tighten the turn and make things worse. Once the turn has developed, the pilot will suffer the illusion of turning in the *opposite* direction when trying to stop the turn. It is unlikely that the appropriate corrective action will be taken, and the turn will continue to develop into a dangerous situation.

Flicker Vertigo

In addition to spacial disorientation (balance organ confusion), there is another form called *flicker vertigo*. This is perhaps the strangest and least-known form. It can result from a light flickering at four to twenty times a second, and may produce unpleasant and dangerous reactions in some people. These reactions include, nausea, dizziness, unconsciousness and even something that is similar to an epileptic seizure.

Flicker vertigo can occur when sunlight passes through the rotor disc and casts a flickering light in the pilot's field of vision. Not very much is known about the dangers of this condition. It is suggested that if the pilot becomes aware of insecure feelings while experiencing flicker conditions, the helicopter should be turned to avoid the effect.

White-Out (Snow Blindness)

The ability to cope in white-out conditions varies with the type of helicopter. The inherent qualities of stability and recovery response certainly influence the degree of intensity of white-out in which the pilot can operate.

Most helicopter pilots with winter flying experience will be aware of the difficulties of landing in large open areas with little reference after a fresh snowfall has whitened the terrain to an even tone. The problem is not significant when clear skies prevail; sufficient light and shadow contrast provides adequate reference. In heavy overcast conditions, however, the problem is increased, particularly if precipitation or low cloud restricts the horizon reference.

Probably the most difficult condition is when the sky is obscured by an even light overcast and when light precipitation is falling. This situation produces a glare that is reflected in all directions. It obscures all shadow contrasts, and relief is almost impossible to detect, even within a foot or two of the ground. This is the condition that produces snow blindness most readily.

Under these conditions, the helicopter pilot may be successful in making a normal approach and descent, particularly if a nearby hedge or tree line is used as a positive reference. The problem arises as the helicopter settles close to the ground. At this level, and at any speed below 10–15 kt (11–17 mph), any loose or powdery snow will blow up in front of and around the helicopter. This great cloud of swirling snow would not be too great a problem if the horizon were clearly distinct beforehand. On a hazy day, or when there is no near reference to trees or contrast, control can be lost easily.

At night, only a small amount of light falling snow can be enough to thoroughly confuse the helicopter pilot.

Grey-Out

Grey-out in a helicopter is no different to that experienced by seaplane pilots when flying low over water in conditions of poor visibility. This occurs in rainstorms or in low ragged-ceiling conditions.

In these cases, the grey of the water and the grey of the sky merge in the haze of the horizon. Under bad weather conditions, the helicopter pilot will tend to fly lower, since this brings the horizon closer and reduces the amount of haze between the helicopter and the horizon. Moisture and condensation on the windshield add to the difficulties.

At these low levels, a further reduction of visibility may force the helicopter pilot inadvertently into the water.

Water Effects

There are several conditions where water can present a problem. Glassy still water affects the helicopter pilot in the same way as it does the seaplane pilot. The only way to judge height above the surface is by close reference to the shoreline.

Other problems are encountered when hovering, or when flying low and slow, over large areas of water with an agitated surface. The aircraft instruments are of little use in this case, but a log in the water or even a boat will provide a useful reference. It should be remembered, though, that a small boat or rubber dinghy will be blown along by the downwash from the helicopter.

AIRPORTS AND HELIPORTS

As helicopters operate in the same airspace as aeroplanes, helicopter pilots must be familiar with fixed-wing procedures. Airport and heliport operations require constant effort on the part of the helicopter pilot to spot and avoid other aircraft.

Learning about airports and heliports is an important aspect of your training.

Runway Numbers

Each runway is assigned a number, which is determined from its *magnetic* direction (usually rounded off to the nearest 10 degrees). For example, runway 02 is 020 degrees magnetic; runway 27 is 270 degrees magnetic. The number is usually displayed on the approach end of the runway in large numerals that are easily read from the air. If parallel runways exist, a suffix letter – 'L' (left) or 'R' (right) – is provided to differentiate between the runways. Some large airports have three runways in operation, in which case, the centre runway has the letter 'C' as a suffix.

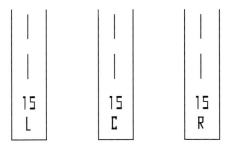

Runway numbers.

Because runways are numbered in relation to magnetic north, not true north, the magnetic compass in the helicopter should agree with the runway designation (within 5 degrees either way) when lined up with the runway. Wind directions are also reported with reference to magnetic north, so a comparison between wind and runway directions can easily be made.

The term *active runway* refers to the actual runway in use at a particular time. This is normally determined by the wind direction.

Heliport Markings

There are several recommended standard markings for heliports; the most common are shown overleaf. The symbols should be enclosed by a white line designating the boundary of the landing area.

Helicopter Landing Area

Recommended Marking
for Civil Heliports

Some Civil and Military
Heliports May Be Marked
With This Symbol

Recommended Marking
for Closed Heliports

Recommended Marking
for Hospital Heliports

Heliport markings.

Airport Elevation

Airport elevation information is important to the helicopter pilot. It is measured at the highest usable landing surface on the airport, and is printed on the navigation charts and aeronautical maps. It is reported as *feet above mean sea level (amsl)*. Prior to take-off, the pilot will set the current altimeter setting, as given by air traffic control, in the sub-scale window on the instrument.

Airport elevation is given in feet above mean sea level.

Windsock

The oldest and most common wind indicating device is the windsock. This is simply a conical sleeve made from durable material and attached by means of a swivel to a post in the ground. When the wind blows through the large end of the cone, it causes the small end to stand out and point *downwind*. The amount of extension can give an indication of the wind strength.

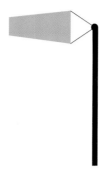

Windsock indicates wind direction.

Operations

Helicopter pilots should be taught to check approach and departure paths prior to take-off or landing. The use of landing lights will often make the helicopter more visible in conditions of reduced visibility.

During all operations, the pilot must maintain an awareness of blind spots, which are inherent in the design of most aircraft. Clearing turns should be employed to expose the airspace that has been hidden by the blind spots of the helicopter.

EMERGENCY PROCEDURES

System failures in modern helicopters are quite rare, but like all mechanical devices, helicopters can go wrong. By obtaining a thorough knowledge of the helicopter and its systems, you will be in a much better position to handle any emergency that does occur.

Autorotation

The most common reason for entering autorotation is an engine failure. This is indicated by one or all of the following:

- A sudden yaw.
- A decrease in engine and rotor rpm.
- The absence of engine noise.
- The loss of height.

Autorotation is made possible because the *freewheel unit* allows the main rotor system to be disconnected from the engine drive system whenever the engine rpm is less than the rotor rpm. In this situation, the main rotor blades are driven solely by the upward flow of air through the main rotor disc. As they continue to rotate, they also drive the main rotor gearbox, which in turn drives the tail rotor. Thus, the main rotor stores energy, which, if used correctly, is available to cushion the engine-off landing.

Several factors affect the rate of descent in autorotation:

- Density altitude.
- Gross weight.
- Rotor rpm.
- Airspeed.

Your primary control of the rate of descent is airspeed. Higher or lower speeds are obtained with the cyclic pitch control, just as in normal powered flight. Autorotative descents can be near vertical at low airspeeds and cover only short distances. Alternatively, an airspeed can be used that produces the minimum rate of descent or maximum horizontal distance.

The technique used for autorotation depends on the height and speed of the helicopter at the time of entry. Obviously, when the autorotation begins from a climb or level flight, the degree of success will be improved if it is initiated from a point outside the marked areas of the height/velocity diagram. The diagram is not as restrictive if the helicopter is already in a descent.

Each type of helicopter has a specified airspeed for the most efficient rate of descent. This speed combines the best glide angle with the slowest rate of descent. The specific airspeed for autorotation for each helicopter type is established on the basis of average weather and wind conditions, and normal loading. When the helicopter is operated at high all-up weights and high density altitudes or gusty wind conditions, best performance will be achieved from a slightly increased airspeed in the descent. For autorotations at low density altitudes and light loadings, best performance will be achieved from a slight decrease in normal speed.

Normally, the autorotation is terminated with a flare to slow the forward speed, reduce the rate of descent and permit a touchdown at low, or zero, speed.

Entering Autorotation

Begin the autorotation by lowering the collective pitch lever to the fully-down position. This reduces the pitch and drag on the main rotor blades, allowing them to continue turning. During practice autorotations, you should keep the rpm in the green band by use of the throttle until the collective lever is fully down. Then reduce the engine rpm by closing the throttle to split the 'needles'.

As the collective lever is lowered, the helicopter should be held in a level attitude with the cyclic stick. At the same time, pedal should be applied to prevent yaw.

An autorotation can be made at airspeeds ranging from zero up to the maximum glide angle speed. If the pilot allows the airspeed to slow down to zero, a near-vertical descent at a high rate will result. At approximately 55 kt (60 mph), the minimum rate of descent should be achieved. If the airspeed is increased or decreased further, the rate of descent will increase. Whenever possible, the pilot should use the airspeed to give the minimum rate of descent (maximum time in the air) in autorotation.

During the descent, turns are normally made using the cyclic stick only. On some helicopters, pedal pressure during a turn may cause the nose of the helicopter to pitch down due to a loss of airspeed, especially when left pedal is applied. Normally, enough right pedal pressure is applied to maintain balance as power is reduced, and then the pedal is held in that position during turns.

Throughout the descent, the pilot should continue to monitor rotor rpm to ensure that they remain inside the permitted operating band. Because of the higher aerodynamic loads imposed during turns, the pilot must be aware of, and expect, an increase in rotor rpm. The amount of increase depends on the tightness of the turn and the gross weight of the helicopter. If the rotor rpm increase, the pilot should gently raise the collective lever slightly, just enough to keep them in the green band.

If the autorotation is initiated on the climb out or approach to landing, there may not be sufficient time or height for extensive manoeuvring. Under these circumstances, the helicopter is normally landed straight ahead.

Autorotations started at low heights mean that the collective lever must be handled with care and lowered as necessary to maintain rotor rpm, but with discretion to avoid a high rate of descent near the ground.

Autorotative Landing

As the helicopter descends toward the ground, the pilot must consider the landing/touch-down phase. The technique used will depend primarily on the airspeed of the helicopter as it approaches a point approximately 100 ft from the ground (Position 3). At this point, the flare is started by applying rearward cyclic pressure. This reduces forward airspeed and decreases the rate of descent. Heading is maintained with pedals. When forward motion drops to the desired ground speed (Position 4), gently check up on the collective lever and move the cyclic stick forward to level the helicopter for touch-down. The height at this time should be about 8 ft, depending on the manufacturer's recommendation. Be careful, at this height, to avoid nose-high/tail-low attitudes. Allow the helicopter to sink, increasing collective lever to cushion the touch-down and keeping straight with pedals (Position 5).

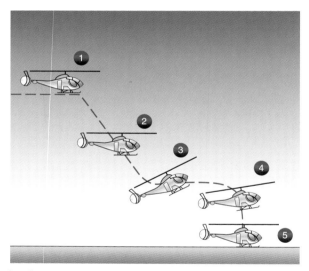

Autorotative landing.

Autorotation from the Hover

Power failures in the hover are practised so that you make the correct response automatically when confronted with a power failure while hovering. In the hover, the pilot is committed to landing on the ground directly beneath the helicopter.

If the helicopter is moving sideways or backward, the movement must be stopped before touch-down. In all cases, the helicopter must be kept in a level attitude by means of the cyclic stick.

An engine failure will be apparent by a sudden yawing to the left due to reduced torque. Immediately, the pilot should apply enough right pedal to control the yaw. Initially, the collective should be held steady because the helicopter will remain in the hover momentarily due to the inertia of the main rotor system.

As the helicopter begins to settle, the collective lever should be raised to cushion the landing. After landing, the collective lever should be lowered smoothly to the fully-down position and the cyclic held neutral.

Vortex Ring (Settling With Power)

Vortex ring is a condition where the helicopter descends vertically at a high rate, even though power is used in an attempt to prevent the loss of height. The term 'settling with power' arises from the fact that the helicopter keeps settling, despite full power being applied.

Certain conditions must exist before this situation occurs:

- A high rate of descent.
- A low forward speed.
- Power on.

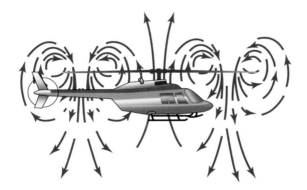

Vortex ring.

Under these conditions, the induced flow down through the main rotor disc becomes equal to the upward flow of air caused by the rate of descent – the net result is thrust. The helicopter actually descends in its own main rotor downwash at a rate that can approach 3,000 ft/min. A fully developed vortex ring state is characterized by an unstable condition, in which the helicopter experiences uncommanded pitch and roll oscillations, and there is little or no cyclic stick authority.

Situations conducive to vortex ring include:

- Attempting to hover out of ground effect above the helicopter's hover ceiling.
- Attempting to hover out of ground effect without maintaining precise altitude control.

- Making downwind and steep power approaches, in which the airspeed is allowed to fall to almost zero.

When recovering from a vortex ring condition, the initial temptation is to try to stop the descent by increasing the collective pitch. However, this only results in increasing the stalled area of the main rotors, thus raising the rate of descent. Recovery is accomplished by increasing forward speed first, followed by partially lowering the collective pitch. After a positive speed increase is observed, and only then, power can be increased to enable the helicopter to climb away.

Retreating Blade Stall

Retreating blade stall is caused by too much forward speed in relation to rotor rpm. Normally, this condition can be avoided by respecting the VNE (velocity never to be exceeded) speed as specified by the manufacturer.

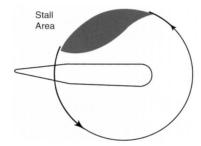

Retreating blade stall.

In forward flight, the relative airflow across the advancing side of the rotor disc is higher due to the forward speed of the helicopter, while the relative airflow on the retreating side is lower. This dissymmetry of lift increases as forward speed rises. To generate the same amount of lift across the rotor disc, the advancing blade flaps up, while the retreating blade flaps down. This causes the angle of attack to decrease on the advancing side (reducing lift) and increase on the retreating side (increasing lift).

Retreating blade stall is a major factor in limiting a helicopter's maximum forward speed. Its development can be felt by a low-frequency vibration, pitching up of the nose and a roll in the direction of the retreating blade.

Situations conducive to retreating blade stall at high forward airspeeds are:

- High all-up weight.
- Low rotor rpm.
- High density altitude.
- Turbulence.
- Steep, abrupt turns.

As altitude increases, higher blade angles are required to maintain lift at a given airspeed. Thus, retreating blade stall is encountered at a lower forward airspeed at altitude.

Correct recovery from retreating blade stall requires the collective lever to be lowered first, which reduces the blade angles. Then rearward cyclic can be used to reduce forward speed.

Ground Resonance

Ground resonance is a phenomenon usually associated with fully articulated rotor systems. This condition can cause a helicopter to self-destruct; it occurs when the helicopter is in contact or partial contact with the ground.

If the helicopter is allowed to touch down firmly on one side, the shock is transmitted to the main rotor system and may cause the rotor blades to move out of their normal relationship with each other. This movement occurs along the drag hinge. As a result, a vibration could occur that, if sympathetic with the inherent vibration, could amplify and resonate the helicopter to destruction.

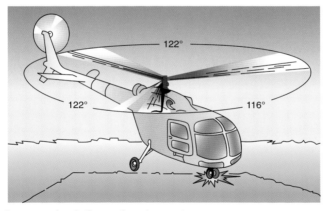

A firm landing can shock the main rotor system.

The corrective action if flying rpm are available is to increase power and lift the helicopter off the ground. If flying rpm are not available, close the throttle and shut down immediately.

This situation does not occur in rigid or semi-rigid rotor systems because there is no drag hinge. Rigid skid-type landing gear is not as prone to ground resonance as skids with dampers or wheels.

Dynamic Roll-over

Dynamic roll-over is the tendency of a helicopter to roll around one of its skids until its critical roll-over angle is reached. This usually occurs when lifting off from a slope, but it can happen on level ground.

There are several factors that can contribute to dynamic roll-over, the main one being incorrect take-off or landing technique. Whatever the cause, if a skid becomes a pivot point, dynamic roll-over is possible if you do not use the proper corrective technique. Once started, it cannot be stopped by applying opposite cyclic stick alone, because the main rotor thrust vector and its moment follow the helicopter as it continues to roll. Lowering the collective pitch lever is the most effective way to stop it developing further.

Low Rotor RPM and Blade Stall
The relationship between rotor rpm and the coning angle is most important for the reasons outlined in Section 1. If you let rotor rpm decay to the point where all the main rotor blades stall, the result is usually fatal. The danger of low rotor rpm and blade stall is greatest in helicopters with low blade inertia. Simply operating the throttle the wrong way or pulling more collective pitch than power available is enough to make the rpm begin to fall.

As rotor rpm reduce, the rotor blades try to maintain the same amount of lift by increasing pitch. As the pitch increases, drag increases. This, in turn, requires more power to keep the blades turning. When power is no longer available to maintain rpm, the helicopter begins to descend. This changes the relative wind and further increases the angle of attack. At some point, the rotor blades will stall unless rotor rpm are restored. Even though there is a safety factor built in to rpm limits by the manufacturer, whenever rotor rpm fall below the green limit, and you have power, simultaneously open the throttle and lower the collective lever. If you are without power, lower the collective lever and apply a little rearward cyclic pressure.

Partial Power
Manifold pressure is a reliable indication of engine performance. A loss of manifold pressure normally indicates a loss of power.

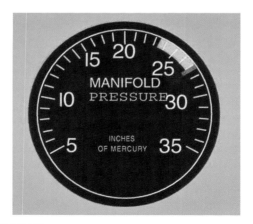

Manifold pressure gauge.

Partial power at altitude usually gives the pilot an opportunity to evaluate the cause and possibly rectify the problem. Turning on a fuel boost pump, verifying that the fuel mixture is fully on, and making sure that the magneto switch is set to 'BOTH' may help in restoring power. If the power cannot be restored, a precautionary landing should be carried out.

It is always wiser to make a precautionary landing than to compromise safety.

Alternator Failure

Malfunctions in the electrical power supply system can be detected by the periodic monitoring of the ammeter. A broken or loose alternator drive belt, or a faulty wire are the most common reasons for alternator failure.

Problems of an electrical nature constitute an emergency and should be dealt with immediately. When evaluating electrical problems, the pilot should remember that the engine electrics are powered by magnetos and are not dependent on the helicopter's electrical system or the battery – except for starting.

Electrical problems normally fall into two categories:

* Excessive charge rates.
* Insufficient charge rates.

After starting and heavy electrical usage, the battery condition may be low. This will cause it to accept a high charge rate during the initial part of the flight. However, after 30 min or so, the ammeter should be indicating less than two needles' width of charging current. If the charge rate remains above this on a long flight, the battery will probably overheat, causing the electrolyte to evaporate at an excessive rate.

Electronic components in the electrical system can be affected adversely by a higher-than-normal voltage. To prevent this possibility, the alternator should be shut down. In this event, minimize the drain on the battery by turning the battery switch to 'OFF', since it can only supply the electrical system for a limited period of time. Terminate the flight as soon as practicable.

If the ammeter indicates a continuous discharge in flight, the system may be receiving insufficient electrical power. If it shows a discharge with only the essential equipment in use, alternator shutdown may be required. To check whether or not the system needs to be shut down, the pilot should watch the ammeter as the alternator is turned off. If the ammeter indicates less discharge, the system should be left off.

If the alternator becomes inoperative, the battery will supply power to all electrical systems, but only for a limited time.

If all the electrical power is lost or turned off, the pilot must consider how the remainder of the flight will be affected. Pitot/static instruments (altimeter and airspeed indicator) will continue to operate, as will the magnetic compass. Communications and navigation equipment will not function. All interior and exterior lighting will be inoperative. Rotor and engine tacho meters, and the manifold pressure gauge will operate as normal. Electrically operated instruments, such as engine oil temperature/pressure, cylinder head temperature, fuel pressure/quantity will not work, neither will the fuel boost pump. Radio transmissions and the landing light should be used sparingly, since they draw large electrical loads from the battery.

Battery

Insufficient battery power is generally caused by one of two problems: either the battery switch was left on after the helicopter was parked, or the battery or electrical system has malfunctioned.

High Engine Temperature

A high cylinder head temperature may be caused by a dirty or inoperative cooling fan, a broken shroud or merely hovering for a long time in high outside temperatures. If the oil temperature is high, the oil cooler may be blocked or malfunctioning, or the oil quantity may be low or of the wrong grade.

Low Engine Oil Pressure

To operate properly, the engine needs a steady supply of oil in sufficient quantity and at the correct pressure. It is very important to develop the habit of checking the engine instruments periodically, particularly during high power settings. Otherwise, a loss of oil pressure, for example, could go unno- ticed until the engine overheats, runs rough or fails. By the time these symp- toms occur, it is already too late to prevent serious damage to the engine. If the situation is questionable, a precautionary landing should be made.

If a total loss of oil pressure precedes a rise in oil temperature, there is good reason to suspect that engine failure is imminent. In this case, an immediate landing should be carried out.

Fires

In general, fires fall into one of three categories:

- Engine fire during start-up.
- Engine fire during flight.
- Electrical fire during flight.

The action to be taken for each category differs considerably.

Engine Fire During Start-Up
Most fires that occur during engine starting result from over priming. The excess fuel collects in the inlet manifold or runs down into the air intake and ignites when the engine backfires. If this occurs, continue to turn the engine. When the engine starts, increase the speed to 1,500 rpm to draw the flames and accumulated fuel into the engine. Run the engine for a few minutes, then shut it down and inspect for any damage. If the engine fails to start, use a fire extinguisher to put out the fire.

Engine Fire During Flight
In this case, it is best to enter autorotation, place the mixture control to idle cut-off, and the close the main fuel valve. Last of all, turn off the battery master switch before landing.

Electrical Fire During Flight
An electrical fire is usually caused by frayed or broken insulation on the wiring. When a bare wire touches a conductor, it causes a short circuit. Sparks and high current flow cause the insulation to burn. The strong smell of burning insulation is an indication of this type of emergency.

In this situation, the battery and alternator switches, together with all other electrical switches, except the ignition, should be turned off. If the fire is not extinguished quickly, the pilot should prepare for an immediate landing.

Tail Rotor Failure
Tail rotor system failures normally fall into two categories. One occurs because of failure of the power drive section, resulting in the complete loss of anti-torque. The other is due to mechanical control failures that leave the pilot unable to control tail rotor thrust, even though the rotor may still be providing anti-torque thrust.

Failures in the first category include drive shaft failures, tail rotor gearbox failures and even the loss of the tail rotor itself. Any of these cases produces an immediate yawing of the helicopter's nose. The severity of the yaw is proportionate to the amount of power being used and the airspeed. An anti-torque failure with a high power setting at a low airspeed results in a severe yaw to the right. At low power settings and high airspeeds, the yaw is less severe.

If a tail rotor failure occurs, power must be reduced to decrease the main rotor torque. If the failure happens in forward flight, reduce power – in piston-engined helicopters, this means entering autorotation. As the helicopter ceases to yaw, gently rejoin the needles to find a power setting to hold the airspeed at about 55 kt (60 mph). Although the helicopter will not be in balance, it will be possible to continue the flight to an area where a precautionary landing can be carried out. A shallow approach with a run-on landing is the best technique to use.

A mechanical control failure restricts or prevents control of tail rotor thrust. The usual cause is a stuck or broken control rod or cable. Although the tail rotor is producing thrust, it cannot be controlled by the pilot. The amount of thrust being produced depends on the position of the jammed or failed controls. Again, a run-on landing following a shallow approach is usually the best technique to get the helicopter back on the ground.

Loss of Tail Rotor Effectiveness

Unanticipated yaw is the occurrence of an uncommanded yaw rate that does not subside of its own accord and, which, if not corrected, can result in the loss of helicopter control. This uncommanded yaw rate is referred to as *loss of tail rotor effectiveness* (LTE). It occurs to the right in helicopters with a counter-clockwise rotating main rotor.

LTE is not the result of equipment or mechanical problems. It can occur in all single-rotor helicopters at airspeeds of less than 40 kt (35 mph), and is the result of the tail rotor not providing adequate thrust to maintain directional control. It is caused by certain wind azimuths (directions) while hovering, or by an insufficient tail rotor thrust for a given power setting at high altitudes.

In still air, for any given main rotor torque setting, there is an exact amount of tail rotor thrust required to prevent the helicopter from yawing. This is known as *tail rotor trim thrust*.

The required tail rotor thrust is modified by the effects of the wind. Certain relative wind directions are more likely to cause tail rotor thrust variations than others. Wind-tunnel experiments have identified three relative wind azimuth areas that either singly, or in combination, can create an environment conducive to LTE.

Main Rotor Disc Interference – 285–315 degrees
Wind velocities of 10–30 kt (12–35 mph) from the left front will blow the main rotor vortex into the tail rotor. This causes the tail rotor to operate in an extremely turbulent environment. During a right turn, the tail rotor develops varying amounts of thrust as the main rotor vortex moves across the tail rotor disc. Initially, the effect increases the angle of attack on the tail rotor blades, thus increasing thrust. This increase in angle of attack requires a right pedal input to maintain the turn. As the main rotor vortex passes the tail rotor, the angle of attack is reduced, causing a reduction of thrust and an acceleration of right yaw.

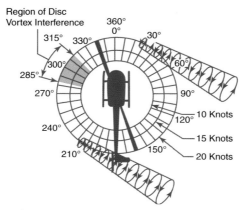

Main rotor disc interference.

This acceleration can catch you out, since previously you were applying right pedal to maintain the right turn. The thrust reduction occurs suddenly and, if uncorrected, can develop into an uncontrollable rapid rotation.

When operating in this region, be aware that the reduction in tail rotor thrust can happen quite suddenly. Be prepared to act quickly with left pedal.

Weathercock Stability – 120–240 degrees

In this region, the helicopter tries to weathercock around into the relative wind. Unless a pedal input is made, the helicopter will start a slow, uncommanded turn either to the right or left, depending upon the wind direction. If the pilot allows a right yaw to develop and the tail of the helicopter moves into this area, the yaw rate can accelerate rapidly. To avoid the onset of LTE in this downwind condition, it is important to maintain positive control of the yaw rate and concentrate on flying the helicopter.

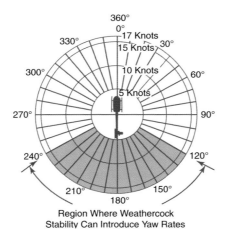

Region Where Weathercock
Stability Can Introduce Yaw Rates

Weathercock stability.

Tail Rotor Vortex Ring – 210–330 degrees

Winds within this area cause a tail rotor vortex ring to develop with an unsteady airflow into the tail rotor. The vortex ring causes variations in tail rotor thrust, resulting in yaw deviations. The effect of all of this is an oscillation of tail rotor thrust. Rapid and continuous pedal movements are necessary to compensate for the rapid changes in tail rotor thrust when hovering in a left crosswind. Holding a steady heading in this area is difficult, but not impossible. High pedal workload, lack of concentration and over-controlling can all lead to LTE.

When the tail rotor thrust being generated is less than the thrust required, the helicopter yaws to the right. When hovering in left crosswinds, you must concentrate on smooth pedal co-ordination and not allow an uncontrollable right yaw to develop. Pilot workload during a tail rotor vortex ring condition is high. Do not allow a right yaw rate to increase.

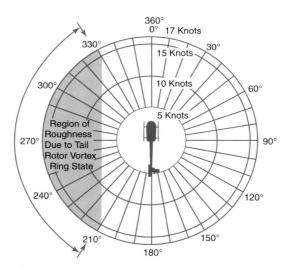

Tail rotor vortex ring.

Reducing the Onset of LTE

There are several actions that will reduce the likelihood of loss of tail rotor effectiveness:

- Maintain maximum allowable rotor rpm. If the main rotor rpm decrease, so does the tail rotor thrust.
- Avoid tail winds below an airspeed of 30 kt (35 mph). If loss of translational lift occurs, it results in an increased power demand and additional anti-torque pressures.
- Avoid OGE operations and high-power situations with an airspeed below 30 kt (35 mph).

- Always be aware of wind direction and strength when hovering in winds of about 8–12 kt (9–14 mph). Any loss of translational lift results in an unexpected high power demand and an increased anti-torque requirement.
- Be aware that if a considerable amount of left pedal is being maintained, enough extra left pedal may not be available to counteract unanticipated right yaw.
- Always be alert to changing wind conditions, especially when operating along ridge lines and near buildings.

Recovery Technique

If a sudden unanticipated right yaw occurs, apply full left pedal and simultaneously apply forward cyclic to increase speed. If the rotation cannot be stopped and ground contact is imminent, an autorotation may be the best course of action.

ABNORMAL VIBRATIONS

Because there are so many moving parts in a helicopter, some vibration is inherent. With experience, you will learn which vibrations are normal and which are abnormal. You need to understand the cause and effect of helicopter vibrations, because abnormal ones cause premature component wear and may even result in structural failure. Helicopter vibrations are usually categorized into low, medium and high frequency.

Low-Frequency Vibrations (100–500 cycles/min)
This type of vibration usually originates from the main rotor system. They can be felt through the controls and the airframe, and have a definite direction of push or thrust. It may be vertical, horizontal, lateral or a combination of these. The direction of the vibration, and whether it is felt in the controls or the airframe, will help the engineer when troubleshooting the source. Causes of low-frequency vibrations include main rotor blade tracking, faulty drag dampers and worn bearings.

Medium-Frequency Vibrations (1,000–2,000 cycles/min)
These vibrations are often associated with the tail rotor drive shaft, engine pulleys, belts and accessories. Causes can range from worn bearings to wrongly adjusted or misaligned components.

High-Frequency Vibrations (2,000 cycles/min or higher)
Normally, high-frequency vibrations are caused by engine, transmission or tail rotor problems. Causes include damaged tail rotor blades, worn bearings and misalignment problems.

All vibrations should be reported immediately to prevent serious damage to the helicopter. If vibrations occur in flight, common sense and good airmanship call for a precautionary landing.

WEIGHT AND BALANCE

All helicopters must comply with the weight and balance limitations laid down by the manufacturer. Operating outside these limits can be fatal. Loading the helicopter above the maximum permitted weight compromises its structural integrity and affects performance. Balance is also critical; on some helicopters, deviations from the CG of as little as 3 in (75 mm) can dramatically change the handling characteristics. Flying a helicopter that is not within its weight and balance limits is unsafe.

Weight

When calculating the weight of the helicopter, you must consider the weights of the crew, passengers, freight and fuel, in addition to the weight of the helicopter itself. The most common terms when computing the weight of the helicopter are:

Basic empty weight The weight of the helicopter with all its equipment, unusable fuel, and full operating fluids, including full engine oil.

Maximum gross weight (maximum all-up weight – MAUW) The maximum permitted total weight of the helicopter.

Useful load The difference between take-off weight and basic empty weight.

Payload The weight of all the passengers, freight and baggage.

Usable fuel The total fuel that is available for flight planning.

Unusable fuel The fuel remaining after an engine run-out test.

Gross weight The sum of the basic empty weight and the useful load.

Weight Limitations

Weight limitations are necessary to preserve the structural integrity of the helicopter. They also help in predicting the performance accurately. Although a helicopter is certificated for a specified maximum gross weight, it is not safe to take-off with this load under all conditions. Factors that affect performance include, high altitude, high temperature and high humidity (high density altitude).

The basic empty weight information for your helicopter, along with basic weight centre of gravity information can be found in the weight and balance schedule. This will be included in the flight manual or will be published separately as part of the helicopter's documentation.

The basic empty weight can vary even for the same model of helicopter, because of differences in the installed equipment. If equipment is fitted or removed at any time, these changes must be reflected in the weight and balance schedule.

Balance

Performance of the helicopter is not only affected by weight but also by how that weight is positioned. It is essential, therefore, to load the helicopter within its laid down centre of gravity limits.

Centre of Gravity

The centre of gravity (CG) is defined as the theoretical point where all of the helicopter's weight is considered to be concentrated. For helicopters with a single main rotor, normally the CG is close to the main rotor mast.

Improper balance of a helicopter's load can result in serious control problems. The permitted limits of the CG are known as the *CG range*. Again, the CG location and CG range are detailed in the weight and balance schedule for every helicopter. Since the fuselage acts as a pendulum suspended from the main rotor, a change in CG will change the angle at which the helicopter hangs below the rotor.

CG position can affect the helicopter's handling.

CG Forward of the Forward Limit

This can occur when a heavy pilot and passenger take off without baggage or ballast aft of the main rotor mast. The situation becomes worse if the fuel tanks are located behind the main rotor mast – as fuel burns, the weight aft of the mast becomes less.

You can recognize this condition when coming to the hover. The helicopter will have a distinct nose-down attitude, and you will have to use excessive rearward cyclic stick movement to maintain a level attitude. You should not continue with the flight because:

- You could run out of rearward cyclic control as fuel is burnt off.
- You may find it impossible to decelerate sufficiently to bring the helicopter to a stop.
- In the event of having to carry out an autorotative landing, you may not have enough cyclic control to flare the helicopter prior to touch-down.

CG Aft of the Aft Limit

This situation usually occurs when lightweight pilots fly without proper ballast. The condition can be recognized as you come to the hover because the helicopter will have a marked tail-low attitude, and you will need plenty of forward cyclic stick pressure. If flight is continued in this situation, you may find it impossible to reach higher cruising speeds through lack of available control movement.

Exceeding the aft CG may occur when:

- A lightweight pilot takes off solo with full fuel located aft of the main rotor mast.
- A lightweight pilot takes off with maximum baggage in the compartment located aft of the main rotor mast.

Lateral Balance

For most helicopters, normally it is not necessary to calculate the lateral CG for routine training and passenger flights. This is because with small helicopters, the cabins are relatively narrow and the optional equipment is located near the centre-line. Helicopter flight manuals usually specify from which seat the helicopter must be flown when operated solo.

Weight and Balance Calculations

In determining whether your helicopter is correctly loaded, you must answer two questions:

1. Is the gross weight less than, or equal to, the maximum allowable gross weight?
2. Is the CG within the allowable range, and will it remain within that range as fuel is burned off?

To answer the first question, simply add the weight of all the items comprising the useful load (pilot, passengers, fuel, freight, etc.) to the helicopter's basic empty weight. Check that the total weight does not exceed the maximum allowable gross weight.

To answer the second question, you need to refer to the loading information in the helicopter's weight and balance schedule or the flight manual.

The following terms are used when calculating a helicopter's CG.

Reference datum The CG is usually described as being so many inches from the reference point. This is an imaginary point arbitrarily fixed somewhere along the longitudinal axis of the helicopter, from which all horizontal distances are measured when making weight and balance calculations. There is no fixed rule for its location.

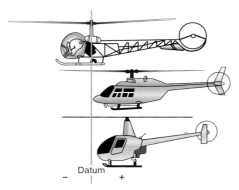

Longitudinal reference datum.

Normally, the lateral reference datum is located at the centre of the helicopter.

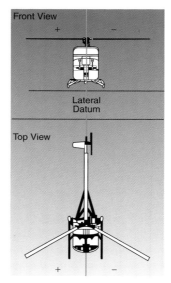

Lateral reference datum.

The locations of all reference datums for any helicopter are established by the manufacturer, and will be defined in the flight manual.

Arm The horizontal distance from the datum to any component of the helicopter is known as the *arm* (sometimes *station*). If the component is located to the rear of the datum, it is measured as a positive number and referred to as inches aft of the datum. Conversely, if the component or object is located forward of the datum, it is indicated as a negative number and referred to as inches forward of the datum.

114

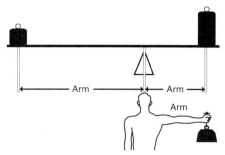

Horizontal distance from datum is known as the arm.

Moment If the weight of an object is multiplied by its arm, the result is known as its *moment*. Moment is also referred to as the tendency of an object to rotate or pivot about a point. The further an object from a pivotal point, the greater its force.

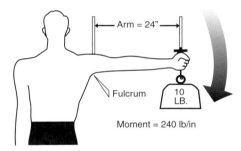

Moment results from multiplying weight by arm.

CG Computation

Since the correct weight and balance of your helicopter is critical to safe flight operations, it is important that you understand how to check it for any loading arrangement. If you had to weigh and measure every item each time you needed to calculate the CG, it would be very time consuming indeed. To simplify this task, the manufacturer includes tables and graphs in the helicopter's flight manual.

To calculate the CG, first you should list the basic empty weight, pilot, passengers, fuel, baggage, etc, together with their respective weights and arms. Then multiply the weights and arms together to find the moment for each item. The helicopter's basic weight and moment are listed in the weight and balance schedule. Add all the weights together to obtain the total weight. Then add all the moments together to find the total moment. To find the CG, simply divide the total moment by the total weight. Compare the total weight to the maximum permitted weight. Check that the CG position is within the certificated forward and aft limits. If there are any discrepancies, you will have to adjust the loading to move the CG back within limits.

Sample CG Loading Calculation

Use the information provided below, which is typical of that found in a helicopter's flight manual, to make a sample CG loading calculation. The longitudinal limits are shown to be variable, with gross weight from 92 in to 100 in aft of the datum. The lateral limits are − 3,200 in/lb to +3,700 in/lb. The maximum gross weight of the helicopter is limited to 2,350 lb. The basic empty weight is 1,495 lb, with a moment of 151,593 in/lb; the pilot weighs 180 lb; the passenger, 190 lb; baggage, 30 lb; and a fuel load of 240 lb. The calculation is as follows:

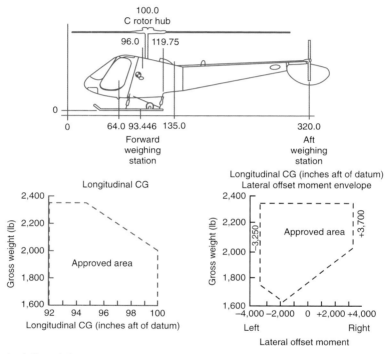

CG calculation data.

Item	Weight (lb)	Arm (in)	Moment (lb/in)
Basic weight	1,495	101.4	151,593
Pilot	180	62.0	11,160
Passenger	190	62.0	11,780
Fuel	240	96.0	23,040
Baggage	30	135.0	4,050
Totals	2,135	201,623	

CG = total moments divided by total weight

= 201,623 divided by 2,135

= 94.44 in aft of the datum

The calculated take-off weight of 2,135 lb is below the permitted maximum 2,350 lb. Next, refer to the longitudinal CG table on page 116. Note that the CG is well within the limits allowed.

The lateral CG calculation is similar to the longitudinal computation, but as the lateral datum is almost always defined as the centre of the helicopter, you are likely to encounter negative CGs and moments in your calculations. Negative values are located on the left side, while positive values are on the right. Normally, the lateral CG will remain inside limits unless the helicopter is loaded abnormally or has been equipped with an external load.

VHF RADIO

For the safe management of all aircraft, both in the air and on the ground, a VHF (Very High Frequency) radio transmitter will be fitted to your helicopter. Many aircraft have two, one as a back-up in case of a malfunction. They operate in the frequency band of 118.0 MHz to 136.975 MHz.

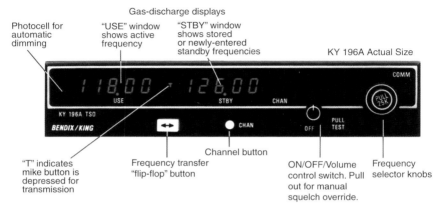

VHF radio controls.

When you turn the on/off/volume knob clockwise to the 'ON' position, the unit will display the frequencies last used in the 'USE' and 'STBY' windows. As with all avionics, it should only be turned on after the engine has been started to protect the solid-state circuitry.

You can select a new frequency in the 'STBY' window by using the frequency selection knobs. The larger knob changes the frequency by increments of 1 MHz; the smaller knob controls changes by increments of 50 kHz when pushed in, and 25 kHz when pulled out. Press the transfer button to activate the new frequency. The newly entered frequency in the 'STBY' window 'flip-flops' with the frequency shown in the 'USE' window.

During your transmissions, a 'T' will appear between the 'USE' and STBY' windows to indicate that the microphone has been keyed.

TRANSPONDERS

All transponders perform the same function, in that they reinforce air traffic control radar echoes so that the controller can identify you positively on his radar screen. If you have an *encoding altimeter*, the transponder can be used to report your altitude as well.

A transponder acts as both a transmitter and receiver, and operates on radar frequencies. It receives ground interrogations at 1030 MHz, which trigger a coded transmission of radar pulses at 1090 MHz.

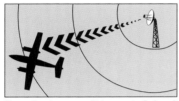

Ground radar sweep "interrogates" aircraft at 10–15 second intervals

Transponder-pulsed transmitter replies to radar station.

A transponder receives signals from a ground radar station and replies with a coded signal.

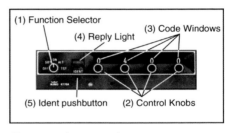

Transponder controls.

Remember always to start your engine before turning on the transponder (this is good advice for all avionics).

The picture above shows typical transponder controls. Turn the function selector (1) to the 'SBY' (standby position). It will take about a minute for the transponder to warm up and become operational. Select the desired reply code by rotating the control knobs (2). When airborne, turn the function selector (1) to the 'ON' position. This sets the transponder to *Mode A* for normal operation. If your helicopter is equipped with an encoding altimeter, turn the function selector to 'ALT'. This is known as *Mode C* for altitude reporting.

When the air traffic controller asks you to 'Squawk Ident', press the ident button (5) briefly. This will cause your helicopter's 'blip' on the radar screen to glow brightly, helping the controller to make a positive radar identification.

During normal operation, the reply light (4) will flash to indicate that the transponder is working properly and replying to interrogations. Sometimes, the reply light will seem to blink almost continuously. This means it is responding to interrogations from several radar stations.

Common transponder codes include:

7700 – only for emergencies.
7600 – signifies communications failure.
7500 – used to report a highjacking.
7000 – general aviation.
0000 – reserved for military use only.

NIGHT FLYING

In many respects, night flying is easier and more pleasant than daytime flying. Less traffic operates at night, and other aircraft are usually easier to see. Also, the atmosphere is generally smoother, resulting in a more comfortable flight.

Important Considerations

On a bright moonlit night, when visibility is good and the air calm, night flying is not a great deal different to daylight flying. The pilot should consider the following factors carefully, however, before making a flight at night:

- Visibility.
- Amount of outside light available.
- General weather situation.
- Proper functioning of the helicopter and its systems.
- Night flying equipment.
- The pilot's recent night flying experience.

Pre-Flight Inspection
Ideally, the pre-flight inspection should be carried out in a well-lit area and with the aid of a torch. The canopy should be checked for cleanliness to prevent dirt from interfering with the pilot's vision.

Lights

Navigation Lights
All aircraft operating between sunset and sunrise are required by law to have operable navigation lights. Usually, these lights are turned on during the pre-flight inspection so they can be checked for serviceability. Navigation lights should be on whenever the engine is running. A red light is located on the left (port) side, a white light on the tail and a green light on the right (starboard) side.

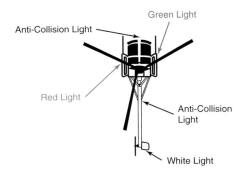

Navigation lights.

Landing and Taxi Lights

All helicopters have landing lights to illuminate the ground when hover taxiing. The landing light is also used during take-off and landing at the pilot's discretion.

Although checking the landing light forms part of the pre-flight inspection, it should not be allowed to remain on longer than is necessary without the engine running. This is because it produces very high drain on the helicopter's battery.

Care should be taken when manoeuvring to prevent the landing light from shining in the direction of other aircraft, as it could impair other pilots' night vision.

Anti-Collision Lights

All recently manufactured helicopters certificated for night flying must be equipped with anti-collision lights to make them more visible to other aircraft at night. The most common type of light is the rotating beacon, which emits red flashes at the rate of about one per second. Also popular are strobe lights, which flash a brilliant red or white light that can be seen over long distances.

Instrument Panel Lights

All helicopters are fitted with some form of lighting system for the instrument panel and/or individual instruments.

Although a pre-flight functional test will have been carried out, a torch should always be carried on night flights to provide an emergency light source. In general, panel lighting is controlled by a rheostat type of switch, which allows the pilot to select a lighting intensity according to his needs.

There are three common types of instrument panel lighting:

Floodlighting A method of illuminating the entire instrument panel from one light source. With this system, a single roof mounted light is used with a rheostat to regulate its intensity. Its beam is directed over both the flight and engine instruments. Floodlighting tends to produce glare if set to high.

Post lighting Individual instruments have their own adjacent light source. Each light beam is directed over the instrument and is shielded from the pilot's eyes.

Internal lighting Similar to post lighting, except the light source is located inside the instrument. Magnetic compasses and radio equipment normally have this type of lighting. It produces the least amount of glare.

Night Vision

The ability to see at night can be greatly improved if the pilot understands and applies certain techniques. If a pilot's eyes are exposed to strong light, even briefly, night vision is destroyed temporarily. For this reason, avoiding any strong light must begin well before a night flight.

It has been found that the adaption required for night vision is decreased most quickly and completely by exposure to white light. Red light is the least detrimental. That said, the use of red light results in the disturbance of normal colour relationships.

Off-Centre Vision

Central vision is normally used to see objects. Under low light conditions, it becomes ineffective. For this reason, a pilot should not look directly at objects. These will be seen more clearly if the gaze is directed slightly above, below or to one side of the object. It has been found that looking about 10 degrees off centre permits better viewing in low light conditions.

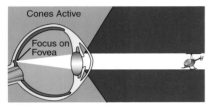

Objects are normally seen with central vision.

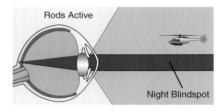

In poor light, central vision is ineffective.

Cabin Familiarization

One of the first steps in preparation for night flying is to become thoroughly familiar with the helicopter's instrumentation and control layout. It is good airmanship to practise locating each control, instrument and switch, both with and without cabin lights. Since the markings on some switches and circuit-breaker panels may be hard to read at night, the pilot must be confident of locating and using these devices in poor lighting conditions.

Airport Lighting

Painted markings at airports are not particularly useful to pilots at night, since they are difficult to see. Therefore, various types of lighting are used to mark and identify different sections of the airport.

Taxiways are marked along their edges with blue lights to distinguish them from runways, which have white lights along the edges. The intensity of runway and taxi lights is controlled by air traffic control and may be adjusted at the request of the pilot.

The threshold of a runway is marked with two or more green lights, while obstructions or unusable areas are marked with red lights.

Engine Start-Up at Night

Caution must be used when starting the engine at night, since it is difficult for people to determine the pilot's intentions. Turning on the navigation lights can help to warn others that the engine is about to be started.

Hover Taxi at Night

Landing lights normally cast a beam that is narrow and concentrated. Because of this, illumination to the side is minimal, so taxi speed should be slower than normal. Initially, judgement of distances is difficult, and it takes some adaption to taxi within the limitations covered by the landing light.

Transition from Hover to Climb

The contrast between day and night flight can be minimized by arranging a night check-out beginning at twilight. This will allow the pilot to take off, fly a circuit and land in a more familiar environment. As darkness increases, the change to night conditions is made gradually.

The pilot should select a point along the departure path for directional reference. During the first night take-off, a noticeable lack of outside visual references is apparent after transitioning. For this reason, a towering type of take-off technique should be used for all night departures.

During the climb out, continue to monitor attitude, airspeed and height to verify the desired profile. The first 500 ft is considered to be the critical period in transitioning from a relatively well-lit area into what appears to be total darkness.

Visual Impressions

During the early stages of night training, most pilots find the initial visual impressions after departing the airport to be vastly different to those that they are accustomed to during daytime flying. Therefore, orientation in the local flying area helps in relating map information to actual terrain and landmarks under night conditions.

The outlines of major towns and cities are clearly discernable at night and, under favourable conditions, are visible from great distances, depending on height.

On clear moonlit nights, outlines of the terrain and other features are dimly visible. On dark nights, however, terrain features are mostly invisible, except in brightly lit, populated areas.

Collision Avoidance

The positions of other aircraft at night can be determined by scanning for navigation lights and anti-collision beacons. Since the arrangement of red and green position lights is the same as that used on ships, the 'red right – returning' mnemonic is applicable. In other words, if the pilot observes red and green navigation lights, with the red light on the right, the other aircraft is approaching. If the white navigation light is visible, the other aircraft is on a heading that will take it away from your helicopter.

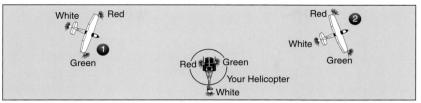

By interpreting the position lights on other aircraft, you can determine whether the aircraft is flying away from you or is on a collision course. If you see a red position light to the right of a green light, such as shown by aircraft number 1, it is flying toward you. You should watch this aircraft closely and be ready to change course. Aircraft nuymber 2, on the other hand, is flying away from you, as indicated by the white position light.

Collision avoidance at night.

Weather

To operate safely at night, the pilot must be particularly attuned to signs of changing weather. A pilot accustomed to daytime flying only is unlikely to be aware that it is extremely easy to fly into overcast at night. This is because the clouds are not easily seen in the dark.

Sometimes, a pilot approaching overcast can detect the presence of cloud because lights in the far distance will disappear. Also, a luminous glow or halo around the navigation lights indicates imminent or actual penetration of cloud.

All pilots should obtain a thorough weather briefing before flying at night, paying especial attention to cloud, fog, icing and precipitation information.

En-Route Procedures

To provide safety margins, the choice of high cruising altitudes is recommended. There are several reasons for this. First, range is usually greater at high altitudes. Second, autorotative distance is greater in the event of engine failure. Third, pilotage and radio navigation are often less difficult.

A major consideration in planning a night flight is to ensure that enough fuel, with adequate reserves, is carried. A useful guideline is to reduce the daytime range of the helicopter by a third when flying at night. This has the advantage that the pilot is not tempted to stretch the range, and the additional fuel can be used to circumnavigate adverse weather.

Special attention should be given to terrain heights shown on the maps to ensure safe clearance.

Emergency Landings

If a forced landing becomes necessary at night, the same procedures recommended for daytime flight apply. If available, the landing light should only be turned on in the final stages before landing.

Approaches and Landings

In some respects, night approaches and landings are actually easier to carry out than in the daytime, since the air is generally smoother, and the disrupting effects of turbulence and excessive cross-winds are usually absent. However, there are a few special considerations that apply to night approaches.

When landing at an airport at night, especially one that is unfamiliar, it is best to make the approach to the lighted runway and then hover taxi to the parking area. The runway lights provide an effective visual clue for judging the night approach. The lights seem to rise and spread laterally as the helicopter nears the touch-down point.

Most pilots use the landing light for night landings. There is a point that should be considered, however, when using this light. The portion of the landing area illuminated by the landing light will seem higher than the dark area surrounding it. This effect tends to cause the pilot to terminate the approach higher than normal. Also, focusing attention on one point in front of the helicopter is poor practice. When using the landing light, the pilot's sighting point should be at least on the forward limit of the illuminated area.

Training for night flying should include landings with and without the aid of the landing light. Proficiency in landing without it requires practice to achieve consistent, accurate touch-downs.

3 AIR EXERCISES

GENERAL NOTES FOR STUDENT HELICOPTER PILOTS

This study guide has been prepared to supplement the flying and ground tuition you will receive from your flying instructor. It is designed to help you understand more fully your instructor's briefings and in-flight demonstrations.

Each exercise does not necessarily represent one flying lesson. Some exercises require several flights, and sometimes more than one exercise will be covered in one lesson. Because of this, you should always be ahead in your reading.

Your instructor will assume that you have read the relevant exercise(s) prior to attending your flying lesson.

This section provides a progressive series of air exercises, together with an overview, in which the helicopter pilot is required to be proficient. It covers all the main considerations that will be taught during full and pre-flight briefings.

Initial flights will be confined to a particular exercise, but as you progress, revision of previous exercises will be included, as well as new, more advanced exercises.

A full briefing will be given before any new exercise is taught in the air. As the name suggests, this briefing will cover the subject in detail. It may take up to an hour to deliver. During the briefing, the lessons learnt in ground school will be linked to the practical aspects of flying.

A pre-flight briefing will be given just before each flight. As well as being a résumé of the main points of the air exercise, it will include information that will affect the flight, such as weather, airfield state, etc.

After every lesson, there will be a post-flight discussion. This will be a review of the air exercise and will be used to amplify or clarify any special points or difficulties. This consolidates the exercise as a whole.

FAMILIARIZATION WITH THE HELICOPTER AND AIR EXPERIENCE

You will be introduced to the training helicopter, its layout and systems. You will use a check-list to carry out a pre-flight inspection supervised by your instructor.

The air experience flight serves to introduce you to the new sensations of helicopter flight and allows the instructor to show you the local flying area. Once back on the ground, your instructor will make sure that you are fully briefed and conversant with all the helicopter checks and drills.

Your instructor will brief you fully on the safety procedures necessary for your helicopter. The two most important points to remember when approaching a helicopter are:

1. Only approach in the sector where the pilot can see you.
2. Do not enter the rotor disc area until you receive positive clearance.

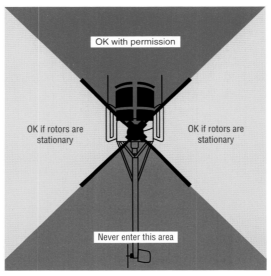

Safe approaches to a helicopter.

EFFECTS OF CONTROLS

Before you can begin to fly a helicopter, it is necessary to understand fully the effects of each control.

Airmanship

During this lesson, the helicopter will be climbing and descending. Therefore, it is of the utmost importance that you keep a good lookout at all times. As well as maintaining the lookout, you will be expected to keep a check on your position within the local area, and make routine checks of engine temperatures and pressures.

The Controls

The Cyclic Stick

This controls the helicopter in the horizontal plane. There is no 'feel' to it, and it is not self-centring. Movement of the cyclic stick in any direction will cause the main rotor disc to tilt in the same direction. This, in turn, changes the attitude of the helicopter. Therefore, forward movement of the cyclic stick causes the disc to tilt forward and the helicopter to adopt a nose-down attitude. Similarly, movement of the cyclic stick to the left (port) will result in the helicopter turning (banking) to the left.

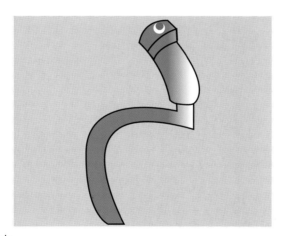

The cyclic stick.

The Collective Pitch Lever

This controls the helicopter in the vertical plane. Raising the collective pitch lever increases the pitch on all the main rotor blades by the same amount at the same time, i.e. collectively. This causes an increase in rotor thrust, resulting in the helicopter entering a climb. Increasing the pitch also increases rotor drag, which causes the rotor speed (rpm) to decay. Lowering the collective lever will have the reverse effect.

129

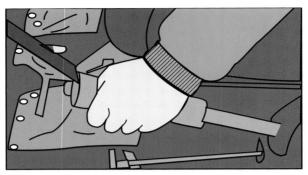

The collective pitch lever.

The Twist-Grip Throttle

Situated on the end of the collective pitch lever, the twist-grip throttle controls engine rpm. As the collective pitch lever is raised and the engine rpm start to fall, the throttle must be opened to maintain the required rpm. As the throttle is opened, increasing torque will cause the helicopter to yaw, which must be counteracted by pedal movement. Since it is always necessary to open the throttle to maintain rpm whenever the collective pitch lever is raised in powered flight, a cam is placed between the lever and the fuel supply unit. As the lever is raised, the cam operates, and extra fuel is delivered to the engine to compensate for the increase in rotor drag and to help maintain rpm.

All lever movements will cause power changes, so yaw pedal will be needed to maintain the heading. In practice, the mechanical cam system is not perfect, and some variations in rpm can be expected as the collective pitch lever is operated. These must be corrected with the throttle.

The Anti-Torque Control (Yaw Pedals)

The pedals are very sensitive and are used in forward flight to keep the helicopter in balance. Whenever power is increased, left pedal must be applied to maintain balance. When power is decreased, right pedal must be applied. Allowing the helicopter to be flown out of balance causes airspeed errors, because the pitot tube is masked from the airflow.

Further Effects of the Throttle and Collective Pitch Lever

At some time during the lesson, your instructor will demonstrate an autorotation. This is achieved by lowering the collective pitch lever progressively and initially maintaining rpm. When the lever is finally down as far as it will go, the throttle has to be closed to keep the rotor rpm in the green section of the gauge. The autorotative state occurs when a needle split is achieved, i.e. the main rotor is freewheeling.

The rate of descent increases as the lever is lowered until it reaches a maximum as the helicopter settles in autorotation.

Frictions

To make flying less tiring, frictions are provided on some controls. The frictions should be adjusted during the pre-take-off checks to the point where the controls do not move of their own accord due to vibration, or in the case of the collective pitch lever, under its own weight. The helicopter is normally flown with frictions off.

Instruments

Of all the instruments, two warrant special mention.

Manifold Pressure Gauge

This gives an indication of engine power. The scale of the gauge is read in inches of mercury.

The manifold pressure gauge.

The RPM Gauge

This indicates both engine rpm (long needle) and rotor rpm. When the clutch is engaged and the engine is driving the main rotor, the two needles will be superimposed. If there is a difference in engine and rotor speeds, e.g. in autorotation, the needles will be split.

Although the rpm gauge is a single instrument in many machines, the Robinson helicopter has separate instruments for engine rpm and rotor rpm.

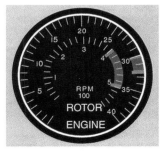 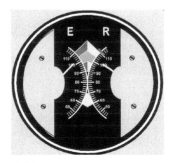

The rpm gauge.   Robinson rpm gauge.

The Effect of a change of disc loading You will be shown how the rotor rpm will rise with an increase in positive G, and decrease if negative G is applied.

The effect of a change of airspeed Your instructor will demonstrate how airspeed affects rotor rpm:

- Airspeed increases, rotor rpm increases.
- Airspeed decrease, rotor rpm decreases.

ATTITUDE AND POWER CHANGES

In this exercise, you will learn the relationship of attitude to airspeed and how to make changes of attitude. You will also learn how to control engine rpm and make changes of manifold pressure.

Airmanship

Lookout

This exercise will involve the helicopter climbing and descending. Therefore, it is very important to maintain a good lookout above and below, as well as at the same height. You must also note your location throughout the lesson. Your instructor will help you by pointing out local landmarks.

Temperatures and Pressures

With lots of power changes during this lesson, it is essential to make regular checks that the temperatures and pressures are in the green sectors of the gauges, and that sufficient fuel remains to continue the sortie.

Positive Hand-over and Take-Over of Controls

During the demonstrations, you will be asked to follow through on the controls. It is important that you do just that and do not override your instructor. When your instructor wants you to take control, he will say, 'You have control.' Then you will take hold of the control(s) and reply, 'I have control.' The order will be reversed when the instructor wants to regain the control(s). Never let go of the controls until your instructor has acknowledged having control.

Attitude and Indicated Airspeed

Starting from cruise flight, you will be shown that there is a set attitude for a given airspeed. You will be shown how to change this attitude and, therefore, alter the airspeed. Due to an effect called *flapback*, which your instructor will explain to you, you will find that as the airspeed changes, the attitude will change for the same cyclic position. Therefore, it is necessary to hold the desired attitude by moving the cyclic stick further during the speed change. You will be required to recognize and maintain these set attitudes so that you can fly at selected airspeeds.

Changing Power at Constant RPM

The height of the helicopter is controlled by the collective lever, which, in turn, controls the pitch of the main rotor blades. As pitch is altered, the engine power – manifold pressure (MP) – will have to be adjusted to maintain constant rpm because of the change in rotor drag. This power change can be effected either by the throttle twist-grip or by the lever operated cam system. It is worth mentioning that the setting up of the cam will vary from helicopter to helicopter. Consequently, its effectiveness will vary. You will be taught two methods of changing power at constant rpm: correlated and uncorrelated.

Uncorrelated Method

If there were no cam system and the collective lever were raised, the engine rpm would decay. To stop this from happening, the throttle is opened a small amount first, which increases power and rpm. Then the collective lever is raised to reduce the rpm to the original figure and increase pitch. This technique is continued until the required amount of power is reached and the rpm is still at the original figure. To reduce power, the collective lever is lowered first, and the corresponding rise in rpm is controlled by closing the throttle slightly. This technique is continued until the desired power is reached.

Correlated Method

Because the cam system will try to maintain constant engine rpm, often the best way to make a power change is to lead with the lever and make any rpm change with the throttle. This is the method that you will probably use most often.

At this stage, it is important that all your control movements are slow and small until you are satisfied that you are correct in all your actions. As you become more proficient, your instructor will show you how to co-ordinate the use of the throttle and lever in a single movement. You will also find that you want to watch the MP and rpm instruments, and nothing else. Your instructor will remind and encourage you to maintain a good lookout as often as possible, by applying a scan sequence, i.e. lookout – instruments – lookout.

RPM Changes at Constant Manifold Pressure

It may be necessary to change the engine rpm during the climb or descent, or when inadvertently you allow them to change during normal flight.

To increase rpm with constant manifold pressure, lead with the throttle. This results in not only an increase of rpm, but also an increase in MP. Then lower the collective lever until MP reduces to the original value; the rpm will rise again.

To decrease rpm with constant manifold pressure, lead with throttle. This results in not only a decrease of rpm, but also a decrease in MP. Then raise the collective lever until MP returns to the original figure; the rpm will decrease further.

If Manifold Pressure is	And rpm is	Solution
Low	Low	Increasing the throttle increases manifold pressure and rpm.
High	Low	Lowering the collective pitch decreases manifold pressure and increases rpm.
Low	High	Raising the collective pitch increases manifold pressure and decreases rpm.
High	High	Reducing the throttle decreases manifold pressure and rpm.

134

STRAIGHT AND LEVEL FLIGHT

Flight training really begins with instruction in the techniques of straight and level flight. The objectives are to point the helicopter in a particular direction, maintain that direction and fly at a predetermined altitude.

The helicopter pilot maintains direction and altitude by controlling the pitch and bank with reference to the natural horizon. This is called *attitude flying*. During training, the pilot learns that there is a fixed attitude and a fixed angle of bank, in relation to the natural horizon, for each flight condition.

The pilot must be aware of the differences between visual flying and instrument flying.

Visual flying simply means that the natural horizon is used as the main reference.

Instrument flying is performed when the pilot refers to instruments for attitude reference.

The emphasis during basic training will be on visual flying.

In straight and level cruising flight, the helicopter will be slightly nose-down and laterally level in relation to the horizon. To maintain this configuration, it is necessary to establish the relationship of the helicopter to the natural horizon. One of the best ways a helicopter pilot can accomplish this is by using the distance between the horizon and the main rotor tip-path plane as a reference. For any given airspeed, the distance will remain the same as long as the pilot sits in the same position in the same type of helicopter.

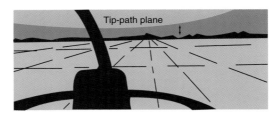

Use the rotor tip-path plane and horizon as a reference.

A straight and level attitude can be maintained by keeping the rotor tip-path plane parallel to the horizon to control the bank attitude, and a set distance above or below the horizon (depending on the airspeed) to control the pitch attitude.

In practising straight and level flight, the pilot learns to maintain a specific compass heading or a heading with reference to outside markers, and to establish a lateral and pitch attitude for level flight.

Attitude Flying

To reach the desired standard, the pilot must learn the techniques of scanning. Develop the habit of keeping your eyes moving continuously between reference points, as well as maintaining a watch for other aircraft. At no time should your concentration be on any one reference.

Several factors may cause the helicopter to move away from the desired attitude. Power changes, turbulence and brief periods of inattention can all cause changes in heading or airspeed. Since all flying is a continuous series of small corrections, the pilot must learn to maintain the correct attitude as closely as possible, and to make smooth, prompt corrections as required. Because the helicopter is highly manoeuvrable, abrupt changes can result in over-controlling.

Corrections should always be made in two steps. First, the attitude deviation is stopped. If the heading or altitude is changing, control pressures are applied to return the helicopter to the level flight attitude. Second, the attitude reference points are adjusted to make a slow correction back to the desired indication. After the corrections are made, the pilot should maintain the attitude reference to attain the desired flight conditions.

Altitude and Collective Lever Movements
The collective pitch control is the primary altitude control. Raising the collective pitch lever increases the pitch angle of the main rotor blades and, through a cam linkage, increases engine power. Both of these inputs cause the helicopter to gain height.

Throttle Control
The twist-grip throttle is mounted on the end of the collective pitch lever. It is used to control engine rpm. If the cam system does not automatically maintain rpm when the collective lever is moved, the throttle must be used to correct engine speed. Rotating the throttle outward increases rpm; inward rotation decreases rpm. The pilot must co-ordinate the throttle and lever movements. Both controls are quite sensitive, so control *pressures* must be used rather than control movements.

The twist-grip throttle control.

Directional Control and Cyclic Movement
The cyclic pitch control tilts the main rotor tip-path in the direction of the desired horizontal movement. In forward flight, moving the cyclic stick to

the left or right will cause a roll (bank) in the respective direction. Moving the cyclic stick forward will cause the nose to drop; similarly, a rearward movement will cause the nose to rise.

Trim

Trim adjustments eliminate the need to apply continuous pressure on the cyclic stick to maintain the desired attitude. Trim is only used to relieve control forces; it is not used to fly the helicopter. The correct procedure for using cyclic trim is to select the required attitude first with the cyclic pitch control, then trim away the forces so that the control remains steady. Trim adjustments should be made after any changes of airspeed and/or power.

Effects of Pedal Movement

The anti-torque pedals are used to control movement around the vertical axis. As power is applied, the helicopter tends to rotate to the right due to torque reaction. Left pedal pressure is used as necessary to keep the helicopter heading in the desired direction. The opposite is true with a reduction in power, i.e. right pedal must be applied to maintain the heading.

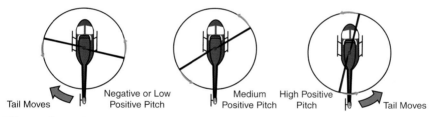

Tail Moves — Negative or Low Positive Pitch — Medium Positive Pitch — High Positive Pitch — Tail Moves

Effects of pedal movement.

Control Co-ordination

As previously stated, the collective pitch control and throttle are used primarily to control engine power, rpm and altitude. The cyclic stick controls heading and bank; the pedals, control yaw.

In some phases of flight, these controls have secondary functions. The secondary function may be so subtle and closely integrated with the primary function that the student pilot may have difficulty relating control movement to helicopter response.

As an example, consider the task of maintaining straight and level flight at a constant power setting. To maintain the desired altitude, the pilot will apply cyclic pressure as necessary to hold the required attitude. Collective pitch will be used to set and maintain the cruise power setting. Co-ordinated use of throttle will be necessary to keep the engine rpm within limits, and pedal pressure will be used to maintain balance. Small height changes or corrections can be made with the cyclic stick. Larger adjustments call for co-ordination of the collective pitch lever and throttle, and, therefore, pedal corrections. Airspeed changes are made by altering the disc attitude with the cyclic pitch control, adjusting the power with the collective and throttle, and maintaining balance with the pedals.

Any control input must be co-ordinated with other control inputs. As the student gains experience, this becomes second nature, and they will be able to control the helicopter precisely and smoothly with seemingly little effort.

Air Exercise

The basic rules to remember are that the *collective controls height*, and the *cyclic controls attitude* and, therefore, *airspeed*. Remember to allow time for the airspeed to stabilize before making further attitude adjustments. Whenever a power change is made, it will be necessary to adjust the pedals to maintain balance (cross-check with the ball) and heading. A good tip is to pick a point as far ahead as possible and keep it positioned on the nose.

Level Flight

To achieve level flight, use the visual horizon primarily to maintain the helicopter's attitude. Cross-check with the airspeed indicator (ASI) to ensure that it is the correct attitude for the required airspeed.

You will practice varying the airspeed between 52 and 85 kt (60 and 100 mph) while maintaining a constant height. Less power is needed to maintain level flight at 52 kt (60 mph) than at 85 kt (100 mph), so it will be necessary to adjust the lever position as the attitude change is made to prevent a climb or descent.

CLIMBING AND DESCENDING

Climbing

When practising climbing, the objectives are to obtain proficiency in establishing the correct climb attitude, setting the correct climb power and trimming out the control forces.

Entering the Climb

From straight and level flight, a climb is entered by applying back pressure on the cyclic stick to select the climb attitude. As the attitude is set, the airspeed gradually decreases and stabilizes at or near the desired climb speed. Power is applied smoothly to the recommended setting, and the pedals are used to maintain balance. Since the attitude has changed, the pilot must make a trim adjustment to relieve the pressure on the cyclic stick.

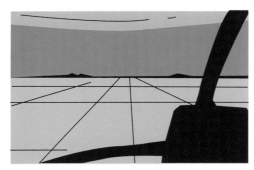

Adjust the attitude by reference to the horizontal and rotor tip-path plane.

The ASI serves as a primary instrument in determining whether the correct climb attitude is being maintained. If the airspeed is higher or lower than that required, a small attitude adjustment should be made by using the natural horizon for reference. Then retrim.

Turning Tendency During the Climb

As power is applied for the climb, the helicopter will tend to turn to the right because of increased torque. The pilot must compensate for this by increasing pressure on the left pedal.

Climb Speeds

In the early stages of training, the instructor will designate a speed as the 'normal' climb speed. This is the speed to be used for climbing exercises.

Cruise climb is used to achieve a satisfactory ground speed while climbing during a cross-country flight. This speed will be somewhat higher than the normal climb speed.

The *best-rate-of-climb speed* is an important performance speed. This airspeed is lower than cruise speed and provides the most gain in altitude per minute.

Therefore, it is the speed utilized to get the helicopter to the desired altitude in the least amount of time. The helicopter will not gain altitude faster at any airspeed higher or lower than the designated best-rate-of-climb speed, because the power required increases.

Level Off from a Climb
To return to straight and level flight from a climb, it is necessary to begin the transition before reaching the required altitude. Generally, the pilot should begin to level off about 50 ft early by applying forward pressure on the cyclic stick to select the level attitude. Then this attitude is held with the aid of outside references. Climb power is maintained until the airspeed increases to cruise speed, at which point cruise power is selected. Finally, cyclic stick pressures are trimmed out. Pedal pressure is applied throughout to maintain balance.

Descending
Descending is practised to learn the techniques required to lose altitude, and to control rates and angles of descent.

Establishing a Descent
To begin a normal descent from straight and level flight, the collective lever is lowered to reduce power, the throttle is used to maintain engine rpm, and the right pedal is pressed to maintain balance. When the helicopter begins to sink, cyclic stick pressure is applied to change the disc attitude for the desired descent speed.

Maintaining the Descent
The ASI, altimeter and heading references are all used during the descent. If an adjustment is required, the pilot should return his attention to outside references, make the attitude adjustment, allow the helicopter to stabilize, then cross-check with the instruments to confirm the correction.

Controlling the Rate of Descent
The rate of descent is controlled with power. An increase in power decreases the rate of descent, while a decrease in power increases the rate of descent. During the descent, the cyclic stick is used to control the pitch and lateral attitude.

Levelling Off from the Descent
To return to straight and level flight, it is necessary for the pilot to begin the transition before reaching the required altitude. At around 50–100 ft above the altitude required, the pilot should begin to increase power smoothly, adjust the nose attitude for level flight and apply left pedal, all simultane-ously. A good scan between outside references and instruments is required to produce accuracy.

Air Exercise
Entering the Climb from the Cruise (A P T)

1. **Attitude** Select the climb attitude with cyclic stick.
2. **Power** Leading with the throttle, smoothly raise the collective lever to increase power to climb setting. Keep straight with left pedal.
3. **Trim** Remove control pressure by trimming.
4. After helicopter settles, make any final adjustments as required.

Levelling Off from the Climb (A P T)

1. **Attitude** At about 50 ft below the required height (more if the rate of climb is very high), select the cruise attitude, but do not lower the collective lever just yet.
2. **Power** When the airspeed has increased, lower the lever slightly and reduce throttle to maintain engine rpm and set cruise power. Keep straight with right pedal.
3. **Trim** Remove control pressure by trimming.
4. Adjust attitude and power as required.

Entering the Descent from the Cruise (P A T)

1. **Power** Lower the collective lever to begin the descent. There is no set power value, since it will depend on the rate of descent required. Maintain engine rpm with throttle, keeping straight with right pedal.
2. **Attitude** Select descent attitude.
3. Adjust power and attitude as required.
4. **Trim** Remove control pressure by trimming.

Levelling Off from the Descent (P A T)

1. **Power** Anticipate the desired height and begin to apply power to cruise setting. Keep straight with left pedal.
2. **Attitude** Select cruise attitude with the cyclic.
3. Adjust power and attitude as required.
4. **Trim** Remove control pressure by trimming.

LEVEL, CLIMBING AND DESCENDING TURNS

A turn is a manoeuvre employed to change the heading of the helicopter. Normally it is qualified by the number of degrees of bank used. As a rule, turns using 15–30 degrees of bank are made in training.

Before starting any turn, the pilot must make sure that the airspace into which the helicopter is going to turn is clear of other aircraft.

Level Turns

Entering a Turn

To enter a turn from straight and level flight, the cyclic stick should be moved smoothly in the desired direction of the turn. How far the helicopter banks will depend on how much lateral pressure is applied. Since some rotor thrust will have been used in the turn, additional power may have to be applied to maintain altitude.

After the turn has been established, outside visual references should be noted and maintained by using the appropriate control pressures. The nose position will appear different during left and right turns. This is because the pilot sits to one side of the helicopter's centre-line. Therefore, a point directly on the pilot's line of sight should be used for reference during turning. The altimeter should be included in the scan to confirm that a constant height is being maintained.

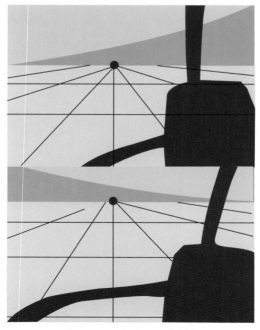

The nose position appears different in left and right turns.

Rolling Out from a Turn

Approximately 5–10 degrees before reaching the required heading, the pilot should apply opposite cyclic stick pressure to stop the turn. As the heading is reached, the helicopter should be in straight and level flight at the desired airspeed.

Climbing Turns

The aim of this exercise is to combine the techniques of climbing and turning. To perform a climbing turn, the pilot should first establish a climb. When the attitude, power and pedal pressure have been set, the pilot initiates a smooth roll to the desired angle of bank with the cyclic pitch control.

The rate of climb will reduce during climbing turns because part of the rotor thrust will be diverted into the turn. Therefore, climbing turns are usually performed at shallow angles of bank.

The desired heading and height are rarely reached at the same time. If the heading is reached first, the turn should be stopped and the climb maintained until the height is achieved. On the other hand, if the height is attained first, the nose should be lowered to cruise attitude and the turn continued on to the required heading. If both the heading and height are reached at the same time, these procedures are carried out simultaneously.

Descending Turns

The aim of this exercise is to combine the techniques of descending and turning. The pilot enters a descent, and when the descent attitude has been established, the helicopter is rolled to the required angle of bank. As with climbing turns, the procedure is performed in two steps. As proficiency is gained, however, the descent attitude and bank can be established in one co-ordinated movement.

As with all manoeuvres, cyclic stick control pressure should be trimmed neutral to maintain the selected attitude.

When using visual references, the nose will look higher in a left turn than in a right turn, although both are performed at the same airspeed.

The nose looks higher in a descending left turn than in a right turn.

143

Power is used to control the rate of descent. The pilot should select the initial descent power setting, then allow the helicopter to settle in a steady rate of descent. If a greater rate of descent is required, power should be reduced further. If the rate of descent is higher than desired, power must be increased slightly.

The rate of descent is higher in a descending turn than in a straight descent with comparable power settings, because the rotor thrust component will be less when the helicopter banks. To compensate, a slight addition to power may be made.

Slip

A slip occurs when the helicopter slides sideways toward the centre of the turn. It is caused by too little pedal pressure in the direction of the turn, or too much in the direction opposite the turn, in relation to the power being used.

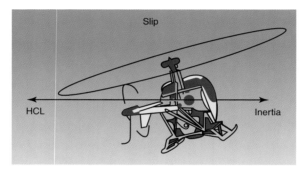

A slip occurs when the helicopter slides toward the centre of the turn.

Skid

A skid occurs when the helicopter slides sideways away from the centre of the turn. It is caused by too much pedal pressure in the direction of the turn, or by too little in the direction opposite the turn, in relation to the power being used.

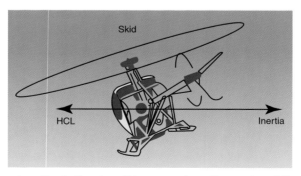

A skid occurs when the helicopter slides away from the centre of the turn.

Air Exercise

Level 15-degree-bank turns, maintaining attitude and angle of bank, will be practised. In a sustained turn, power will have to be increased to maintain height. Turns with the same amount of bank will also be practised while climbing and descending. You will notice that large angles of bank will decrease the rate of climb and increase the rate of descent. Left and right turns will appear to have different attitudes due to the pilot's offset seating position.

BASIC AUTOROTATIONS

Autorotation is possible due to physical laws and because the overrunning clutch (freewheel unit) allows the rotor system to disengage from the engine drive system whenever engine rpm is less than rotor rpm. As the helicopter descends, the upward flow of air through the rotor disc drives the main rotor and the main gearbox, which, in turn, drives the tail rotor. When the helicopter descends in this manner, it is said to be in a state of autorotation.

Attitude Change on Entry and Recovery

On entry into autorotation, the nose will tend to pitch down. The airflow in powered flight flows over the rotor disc and is induced down through it. In autorotation, the airflow rises from underneath and strikes the elevator/tail stabilizer, causing the nose to pitch down.

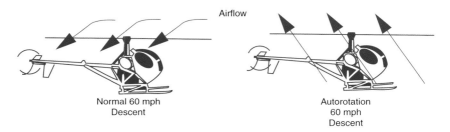

Airflow in autorotation compared to normal flight.

On recovery from autorotation to the climb, the tendency will be for the nose to pitch up. This is more critical, as a nose-up pitch will result in the loss of airspeed. At this stage of the recovery, full power will have been applied, although the helicopter still will have a high rate of descent. The combination of these factors could lead to a dangerous condition of flight known as vortex ring.

Vortex Ring
For a helicopter to experience a state of vortex ring, three conditions must be present at the same time:

- A high rate of descent.
- A low airspeed.
- A high power setting.

Airmanship

The HASEL check is the password to good airmanship and should be carried out prior to each practice autorotation:

146

H   Height sufficient to allow recovery by 500 ft agl if away from the airfield.
A   Area suitable for manoeuvre.
S   Security in the cabin – harnesses, no loose articles, etc.
E   Engine temperatures and pressures indicating normal.
L   Lookout – maintain a good lookout for other aircraft, especially below.

Maintaining a good lookout during the recovery is also important.

In addition, it is a good idea to keep a good check on the wind velocity, and to make sure that the area you are using is really suitable, in case your practice become the real thing.

Air Exercise
The Basic Autorotation
This exercise is practised at 52 kt (60 mph). To enter autorotation, the collective pitch control lever must be lowered and the throttle closed to prevent engine over-speeding. The engine and rotor needles should remain 'joined' until the lever is fully down. Simultaneously with these actions, the nose should be raised smoothly to adopt the 52 kt (60 mph) attitude while remaining laterally level. Lots of right pedal will be required to keep in balance and hold heading.

When the collective lever is fully down, close back on the throttle to idling engine rpm – this is called *splitting the needles*. At this point, the helicopter will be in autorotation.

During the descent, it will be possible to change both speed and direction using the normal control techniques. Increases in speed and disc loading (positive G) will cause an increase in rotor rpm.

To recover from autorotation back to a climb, start at about 300 ft before the minimum height for recovery is reached. A small check up on the collective lever may be required first to ensure that when the engine and rotor needles are rejoined, the engine is not over-sped.

Open the throttle smoothly and positively to rejoin the engine and rotor needles. When the needles are joined, raise the lever, opening the throttle at the same time to maintain engine rpm, until climb power is reached. The nose will tend to pitch up during this large application of power, so apply forward cyclic stick pressure to maintain the climb speed. Keep the helicopter in balance throughout with left pedal pressure.

HOVERING FLIGHT

Hovering is flying the helicopter so that it remains stationary over a point on the ground, at a constant heading and height. The hover is a fundamental requirement in helicopter flying, since it is the prerequisite to safe landings, as well as being a main factor in many operational functions. This exercise requires a high level of concentration and co-ordination. Control *pressures* rather than control movements must be used to avoid over-controlling.

Ground Effect

This is an important factor in helicopter performance, which results from the induced flow through the main rotor disc being impeded by the ground below. It is most effective when the helicopter is close to the ground, and reduces to almost zero at a height equal to the main rotor diameter. It has the effect of increasing performance by reducing the amount of power required to hover.

Hovering Over a Point

To maintain a steady hover over a point, the pilot must look for tiny changes in the helicopter's attitude and height. As soon as these changes are noted, the necessary control inputs should be made before the helicopter starts to move again. To best detect these small variations, the pilot's main area of visual attention needs to be some distance ahead of the helicopter – usually on the natural horizon. Looking too close in, or looking down, will lead to over-controlling.

   Basically, the cyclic stick controls the ground position, the pedals control the heading, the collective lever controls the height, and the throttle controls the rpm.

   To keep the helicopter in a steady hover, the pilot must make small, quick, co-ordinated corrections. These inputs should be applied as necessary, then, as the desired effect occurs, removed, otherwise the helicopter will continue to respond. For example, if the helicopter starts to move backward, a small amount of forward cyclic pressure will stop the movement. However, the forward pressure must be neutralized just before the helicopter comes to a stop, otherwise it will begin to move forward.

   As you gain experience, you will develop a 'feel' for the helicopter. Small deviations will be felt and corrected before they develop; in other words, *anticipation* is the key.

Air Exercise

The aim of this exercise is to teach you how to hover, that is to maintain a given position relative to a point on the ground, at a constant height, heading and engine rpm.

   Normally, the helicopter will hover with the left skid low. This is caused by the corrective action for tail rotor drift. The amount by which the left skid hangs low is dependent on two other factors:

- The lateral centre of gravity.
- The wind strength and its direction relative to the helicopter.

If both seats are occupied, it is probable that the left skid will be only 1 or 2 in (25 or 50 mm) lower than the right skid. On the other hand, if only the left seat is occupied, the skid may be as much as 6 in (150 mm) lower than the right.

In the initial stages of your training, all hovering exercises will be carried out facing into wind. The helicopter will tend to drift downwind if no corrective action is taken.

Therefore, to maintain a position relative to the ground point, the rotor disc must be tilted into wind, which will change the hover attitude.

If the wind velocity changes, it will affect the amount of drift, and a correction must be applied by varying the cyclic stick pressure. Increases and decreases in wind strength will also cause variations in translational lift, making the helicopter rise or fall. These movements must be corrected with power adjustments. In general, the helicopter will tend to climb and move away from any gust of wind.

In still-air conditions, a ground cushion is formed beneath the helicopter, the intensity of which depends on the hover height and the nature of the ground.

In the hover, the helicopter is statically stable, since it will tend to return through its original position if displaced by a gust of wind. It will continue through this position, however, then oscillate about it in increasing amounts. Therefore, the helicopter is dynamically unstable in the hover.

Airmanship

The points of good airmanship relevant to this exercise are:

- Maintain a good, all-round lookout.
- Choose a large area clear of obstructions to practice hovering.
- Pay attention to the wind velocity.
- Monitor temperatures and pressures frequently.
- Take care not to exceed any power limitations.
- Give strict observance to the handing over/taking over of controls.

Hovering

The exercise will usually start with the helicopter heading into wind, with the skids about 4–6 ft above the ground. Each control has a specific job.

The cyclic stick controls the disc attitude and, hence, the position over the ground. Only small movements (pressures) are required. Remember that there will be a slight lag between selecting a new attitude, the helicopter adopting that attitude and the resultant movement.

The collective pitch lever controls the height of the helicopter. Only small movements are required.

The throttle is used to control engine rpm. Only small movements are needed. Remember to check rpm and manifold pressure instruments.

The pedals are used to control the helicopter's heading. They operate in the normal sense, e.g. applying left pedal turns the nose to the left.

To maintain an accurate hover, it is necessary for the pilot to be able to judge whether or not the hover is being maintained. This is achieved by developing a good scan technique, which should include:

- A mid-distance object some 250–350 ft (75–100 m) ahead to gain a general perspective.
- The natural horizon for attitude and heading reference.
- Markers ahead and to the side to determine accurate position and height.
- Frequent reference to the rpm and manifold pressure instruments.

The power required to hover will vary from day to day, as it is affected by the following factors:

The helicopter's all-up weight The higher the all-up weight, the greater the power requirement to maintain a specific hover height.

Hover height As the hover height increases, the power required to hover increases. This increase continues as hover height rises through the height band where the helicopter is said to be hovering *inside ground effect* (hover IGE). Above a hover height of approximately 30 ft, the helicopter is said to be hovering *outside ground effect* (hover OGE), and the power requirement remains constant with any further increase in hover height.

Ground surface The power required to hover over a flat smooth surface is less than that required to hover over a sloping uneven surface, where the ground effect will be reduced.

Wind speed The amount of power required to hover reduces as wind speed increases, due to translational lift.

Density altitude The power required to hover increases as density altitude increases.

The combination of all these factors can have a marked effect on the actual power required to hover.

Common Errors

- Tenseness and slow reactions to movements of the helicopter.
- Failure to allow for lag in cyclic and collective pitch, leading to over-controlling.

- Confusing attitude changes for altitude changes, resulting in improper use of the controls.
- Hovering too low, resulting in occasional touch-down.
- A tendency to stare at a fixed point instead of several reference points, which, when combined, will help to maintain an accurate hover.
- Failure to scan. A technique that involves looking at external references for 75 per cent of the time, and referring to instruments for the remaining 25 per cent of the time is best.

VERTICAL TAKE-OFF AND LANDING TO AND FROM THE HOVER

Normally, landings are taught before take-offs, as they are a direct follow-on from hovering. Unless you can hover steadily, you cannot possibly expect to be able to land with any degree of success. Therefore, a good landing starts from a steady hover.

Landings

Carry out pre-landing checks.

Start with a steady hover, 4–6 ft skid height and pointing into wind. Then, looking well ahead to maintain attitude, lower the collective lever slowly and steadily to make the helicopter descend. At the same time, apply right pedal pressure to keep straight.

Continue the downward movement until the skids touch the ground. Control of engine rpm is by gentle use of the throttle. Maintain a good look ahead to stay level. All movements of the collective lever and throttle produce torque changes, which must be counteracted with pedal pressures.

As the helicopter gets closer to the ground, the left-skid-low problem will become more apparent. Any temptation to try to correct this with cyclic must be avoided. If the left skid touches down first, continue lowering the lever and holding a level attitude until both skids are on the ground. Continue to lower the lever until it is fully down. Control the rpm with throttle, otherwise they could easily exceed their limit. When it is apparent that the helicopter is in full contact with the ground, carry out the post-landing checks:

Throttle Set idling rpm.

Collective lever Check fully down, frictions on.

Cyclic stick Rotor disc level and trimmed.

Pedals Neutral.

During a series of take-offs and landings, an abbreviated check-list may be used.

Throughout the landing sequence, continue to use external references and do not be tempted to look at the ground immediately in front of the helicopter. Above all, make a positive effort to relax.

Mislanding

It is important that neither horizontal movement nor excessive rate of descent be allowed to occur at touch-down. If either exists just before touch-down, the landing must be abandoned by smoothly lifting the collective lever sufficiently to raise the helicopter to a safe hover height. Once back in a steady hover, relax and try again.

Horizontal movement If the helicopter is allowed to contact the ground when moving sideways, even at a low speed, it may be damaged. Touching down with rearward movement could result in damage to the tail. Slight forward movement with no yaw is not dangerous, but you should aim to carry out a true vertical landing.

Excessive rate of descent The danger of touching down with excessive rate of descent is obvious. Aim to make the touch-down positive, but gentle.

Ground Resonance

When landing and taking off, the helicopter should not be allowed to remain lightly in contact with the ground for any longer than is necessary. This is because there is a slight risk that ground resonance – a divergent oscillation about the skids – may develop. If this occurs during the exercise, you must lift off immediately to a safe hover height and allow any oscillations to dampen out.

Take-Offs

Carry out the pre-take-off checks as per the check-list. Ensure the immediate vicinity is clear and make a mental note of the wind velocity. Position the cyclic pitch control so that the helicopter will lift off with no lateral movement – in a strong wind, the cyclic control will be positioned further forward than in calm conditions. Anticipate the eventual pedal position by applying slight pressure to the left pedal.

Increase power smoothly, maintaining rpm until you reach the point where the helicopter is about to break contact with the ground. At this point, transfer your attention to your outside reference point and continue increasing power to make a clean break from the ground.

Continue to climb, maintaining ground position and heading, until the correct hover height is reached. Use the normal, smooth gentle movements to establish the hover.

After settling down in a steady hover, carry out the post-take-off checks:

Controls Normal operation and control forces trimmed out.

Manifold pressure Note power required to hover.

Engine rpm Correctly set.

Temperatures and pressures All within limits.

BASIC TRANSITIONS

The term 'transition' covers all flight from and to the hover.

Hover to Forward Flight

When the helicopter is hovering in still air, the total rotor thrust is equal to the weight. To achieve forward flight, the main rotor disc has to be tilted forward. Now the total rotor thrust must provide both a vertical force to balance weight and a horizontal force in the direction in which the helicopter is moving.

When the helicopter is travelling forward at a uniform speed, the horizontal component, thrust, will be balanced by parasite drag. Since parasite drag increases as the square of the airspeed, the faster the helicopter is moving forward, the greater must be the tilt of the rotor disc to provide that thrust. For level flight, however, the vertical component of total rotor thrust must remain equal to weight. It follows, therefore, that when the helicopter moves forward from the hover, the total rotor thrust must increase.

As total rotor thrust is a function of collective pitch, it would suggest that the collective lever must be raised progressively for any given increase in forward speed. In practice, however, it will be found that for speeds up to 45–55 kt (52–63 mph), depending on the type of helicopter, both the collective lever and power can be reduced progressively. It is only for speeds above this range that collective pitch and power have to be increased.

This gain in rotor efficiency when moving forward is known as *translational lift*. The same effect will occur whenever the helicopter is hovering in wind conditions.

Translational Lift

When the helicopter has established a steady hover in still-air conditions, a certain value of collective pitch, say 8 degrees, will be required to support it in the air. A column of air, the induced flow, will be moving continually down toward the rotor disc, and this downward flow of air must be considered when determining the direction of the airflow relative to the blades. It will be noted that the angle of attack, say 5 degrees, is less than the pitch angle.

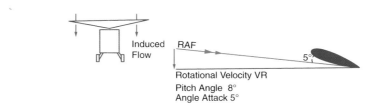

Pitch angle and angle of attack in still air.

The angle of attack depends upon the value of the induced flow. If there were no induced flow, the angle of attack would be the same as the pitch angle.

154

Now consider the effect of the helicopter facing into a 20 kt (23 mph) wind, and assume it is possible to maintain the hover without tilting the rotor disc. The horizontal 'wind' flow of air will blow across the vertically induced column of air and deflect it 'downwind' before it reaches the disc. Therefore, the column of air that was flowing *down* toward the disc will be modified and be replaced gradually by a mass of air that moves horizontally *across* the disc. The main rotor will act on this air mass to produce an induced flow, but the velocity will be greatly reduced. Therefore, an airflow parallel to the rotor disc must reduce the induced flow and so increase the angle of attack.

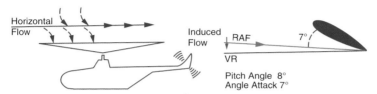

Pitch angle and angle of attack in headwind.

To maintain the hover when facing into wind, however, the disc must be tilted forward. As a result, the horizontal flow of air will not be parallel to the disc, and a component of it can be considered to be actually passing through the disc at a right angle to the plane of rotation, effectively increasing the induced flow. To consider an extreme case, if the rotor disc were tilted at 90 degrees to this horizontal airflow, all of it would be passing through the disc at a right angle to the plane of rotation.

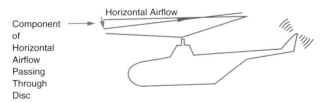

Increase in induced flow due to tilted main rotor disc.

Therefore, the effect of this horizontal airflow across the rotor disc when hovering into wind is to reduce the induced flow, but because the disc is tilted forward, a component of this horizontal airflow will be passing through the disc, effectively increasing the induced flow. Both effects must be taken into consideration when determining the direction of the airflow relative to the rotor blades.

Provided the reduction in induced flow is greater than the component of horizontal airflow passing through the rotor disc, the relative airflow will be nearer the plane of rotation than when the helicopter is in the hover – so the angle of attack will increase.

This means that the collective pitch can be decreased, say to 7 degrees, while still maintaining the *same* angle of attack.

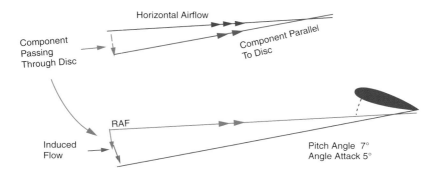

Collective pitch can be reduced while maintaining the same angle of attack.

The lift/drag ratio for this angle of attack remains unchanged, so the total reaction must move *forward* when the collective pitch is reduced. There will be less rotor drag, so rotor rpm can be maintained with less power.

The reduction in induced flow, translational lift, first takes effect when air moves toward the rotor disc at approximately 12 kt (14 mph). The reduction is appreciable at first, and although it continues to reduce as the velocity of the horizontal airflow increases, the rate at which it reduces becomes progressively lower. If induced flow is plotted against forward speed, the graph appears as the left-hand curve shown in Fig 3.21.

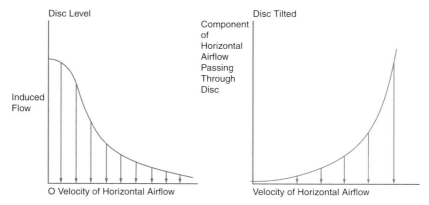

Induced flow vs forward speed with level rotor disc (left); component of horizontal airflow passing through tilted disc (right).

The main rotor disc must be tilted forward to provide a thrust component equal to parasite drag. The latter is low at low forward speed, so only a small amount of tilt is required to provide sufficient balancing thrust. With a small tilt of the rotor disc, only a small component of the horizontal airflow will be passing through the disc at a right angle to the plane of rotation.

Since parasite drag increases as the square of the speed, the disc must be tilted more to provide the necessary increase in thrust. As the velocity of the horizontal airflow approaching the disc increases, the greater will be the component of it passing through the disc at a right angle to the plane of rotation.

If the information given in both graphs is plotted in one graph , it will be seen that the flow of air at a right angle to the plane of rotation decreases at first, then increases, being at a minimum when the two airflows have the same value.

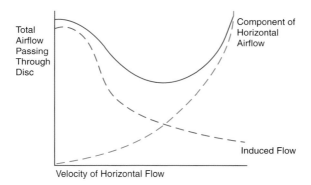

Flow of air at right angle to the plane of rotation.

As the flow of air through the rotor disc decreases, less collective pitch and power will be required to maintain the required angle of attack. When the flow of air through the disc begins to increase again, collective pitch and power must be increased if the required angle of attack is to be maintained.

From Forward Flight to the Hover

If the transition from forward flight to the hover is made by reducing forward speed in lots of little stages, allowing the helicopter to settle at each speed reduction, the collective lever and power changes would be the same as making a transition from the hover to forward flight, but in the reverse sense.

However, the usual method of coming to a hover from forward flight is by executing a *flare*. When this method of reducing speed is used, collective pitch and power changes will differ considerably from those required to produce a more gentle transition.

Flare
To execute a flare, the cyclic stick is moved back in the opposite direction to which the helicopter is moving, the harshness of the flare depending on how

157

much and how fast the stick is moved. The flare will bring about a number of effects, as outlined here.

Thrust Reversal

By tilting the rotor disc away from the direction of travel, the thrust component of the total rotor thrust will now act in the same direction as the fuselage parasite drag. This will cause the helicopter to slow down rapidly. The fuselage will respond to this rapid deceleration by pitching up, because reverse thrust is being maintained while parasite drag decreases. If the pilot takes no corrective action, the rotor disc will be tilted back further, causing an even greater deceleration.

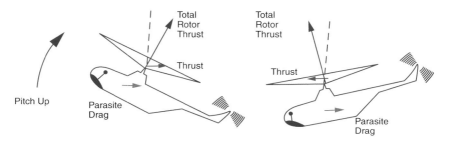

Thrust reversal.

Increase in Total Rotor Thrust

Another effect of tilting the rotor disc while the helicopter is moving forward is to change the airflow relative to the blades. As explained in the section on translational lift, due to the helicopter moving forward, a component of the horizontal airflow passes through the rotor disc at a right angle to the plane of rotation and in the *same* direction as the induced flow. When the disc is flared, a component of the horizontal airflow will *oppose* the induced flow and change the direction of the airflow relative to the blade. This will cause an increase in angle of attack and, therefore, an increase in total rotor thrust.

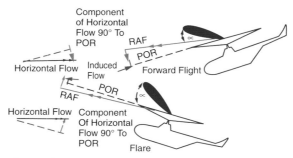

Increase in total rotor thrust.

If no corrective action is taken, the helicopter will climb. If a constant height is to be maintained, therefore, collective lever and power must be reduced.

Increase in Rotor RPM

Unless power is reduced when the collective lever is lowered to maintain height, the rotor rpm will increase. They will also increase rapidly in a flare for two other reasons:

Conservation of angular momentum The increase in total rotor thrust will cause the blades to cone up. The radius of the blades' CG from the axis of rotation decreases, and the blades' rotational velocity rises automatically. Therefore, power must be reduced to maintain constant rotor rpm.

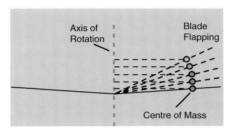

Conservation of angular momentum.

Reduction in rotor drag Rotor drag is reduced in the flare because the total reaction moves toward the axis of rotation as a result of the changed direction of the relative airflow.

Below, the lift and drag vectors have been used to position the total reaction and to show that in the flare, the total reaction moves forward, reducing *rotor drag*. As engine power is used to match rotor drag for a given rotor rpm, if the drag decreases, power must be reduced to maintain constant rotor rpm.

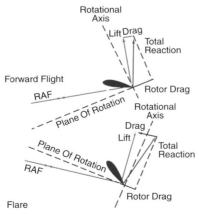

Reduction in rotor drag.

As a result of the flare, the speed reduces rapidly and the flare effects disappear. Collective pitch and power, which were reduced during the flare, must be restored and, in addition, *more* collective pitch and power must be used to replace the loss of translational lift caused by the speed reduction, otherwise the helicopter will sink.

The cyclic stick must also be moved forward to level the helicopter and prevent it from moving backward.

The power changes necessary during the flare affect the helicopter in the yawing plane. Therefore, pedals must be used to maintain heading throughout.

Air Exercise

Before any attempt is made to transition away from the hover, you must ensure not only that the area ahead of the helicopter is clear, but also that no aircraft are approaching to land in the immediate vicinity. This means that you must turn the helicopter in the hover to look in the direction of the approach. This turn is called a *lookout turn*. It is carried out whenever you wish to change ground position or transition away. The first lookout turn of the flight should be to the left to check the power required and pedal availability.

The Lookout Turn to the Left

From a steady hover into wind, check that the area into which you intend to swing the tail is clear. Increase left pedal pressure and slowly yaw around to the left. Concentrate on maintaining ground position by moving the cyclic stick toward the wind and preventing any drift. Continue with this slow yaw to the left until the helicopter has turned through approximately 90 degrees. The cyclic stick will be displaced slightly to the right to maintain ground position. Steady the hover on this new heading, then look in the direction of the approach. With experience, you will be able to look out as you turn, but at this stage, you must turn, then look, otherwise the hover may become unsteady.

Having completed the lookout, look ahead and concentrate on the hover. When steady, release pressure on the left pedal and allow the helicopter to yaw right until the nose is pointing into wind. Remember to move the cyclic stick toward the original position during the turn.

Effects of Transition from the Hover into the Climb

To initiate a transition into forward flight, a slight accelerative attitude should be selected. Several noticeable effects occur during the transition. As these relate mainly to airspeed, they are best observed in light wind conditions. Your instructor will show you as many of these effects as possible in the prevailing wind conditions.

Initial height loss If the collective lever position is maintained, there will be an initial height loss as the accelerative attitude is selected. In the main, this is due to the tilting of the main rotor disc, but also, to a lesser extent, to the loss of ground effect.

Flapback and inflow roll Shortly after the helicopter begins to move forward, there will be a tendency for it to pitch nose-up (flapback), and to roll to the right (inflow roll). The combined effect can be quite marked.

Translational lift At approximately 13–17 kt (15–20 mph), there will be a noticeable increase in translational lift, which causes the helicopter to climb. Normally, this effect is accompanied by a slight buffet.

The initial height loss is prevented by use of the collective lever, while translational lift helps the helicopter to climb. The problems of flapback and inflow roll will be overcome if you select and maintain the required accelerative attitude using visual references.

The Transition into the Climb
Refer to the figure below. While in a steady hover (1), check that the power available (difference between power required to hover and maximum power possible) is sufficient and carry out a lookout turn. Start the helicopter moving forward with the cyclic stick (2). Raise the collective lever as necessary to prevent the helicopter from sinking, and adjust the throttle to maintain engine rpm. The increase in power will require an increase in left pedal pressure to maintain the heading. As you accelerate through effective translational lift (3), the helicopter will begin to climb and the nose will want to pitch up due to increased lift. At position 4, hold an attitude that allows a smooth acceleration toward climbing speed and a commensurate gain in height. As airspeed increases (5), the streamlining of the fuselage will reduce the engine torque effect, allowing a gradual reduction of left pedal pressure.

The transition to the climb.

As the helicopter continues to climb and accelerate to the best-rate-of-climb speed, adjust the cyclic stick to maintain the climb attitude. Ideally, the aim is to achieve 52 kt (60 mph) at approximately 100 ft above the ground.

Common errors include:

- Failing to use sufficient collective pitch to prevent loss of height prior to attaining translational lift.
- Applying power too soon at the beginning of the transition without forward cyclic compensation, causing the helicopter to gain height before acquiring airspeed.
- Assuming an extreme nose-down attitude near the ground when starting the transition.
- Failing to hold heading.
- Failing to maintain proper airspeed during the climb.
- Failing to adjust the throttle to maintain proper rpm control.

The Transition from Straight and Level Flight
The purpose of this exercise is to select and maintain a constant angle of approach from straight and level flight to the hover over a pre-selected point.

The Constant Angle of Approach
This is a straight-line flight path from the point of initial descent to the hover. The angle of approach will depend upon the height from which the descent is begun and the distance from the hover point. Once selected, the angle should be maintained using the collective lever and throttle, while the rate of approach should be controlled with the cyclic stick.

Selecting the Normal Angle
The initial run-in height for the normal approach is 500 ft. The distance from the hover point must be judged by line of sight, by using the top of the instrument panel and the landing point as references for example. A helicopter flying straight and level at 500 ft toward the hover point will be faced with an ever increasing approach angle. This will be apparent by the landing point appearing to move gradually down in relation to the instrument panel.

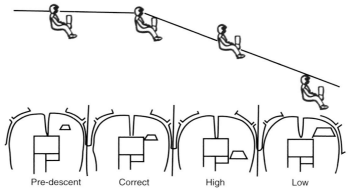

Judging angle of approach by sight picture.

The correct approach angle will be demonstrated to you by your instructor. This 'sight picture' will vary from one student to another, due to differences in seating position, etc., so it is important that you note the positions of the references as your instructor begins his demonstration approach.

Maintaining the Selected Angle

As soon as the correct angle is indicated, the power must be reduced suffi-ciently to prevent any further relative change between the two references. Any change in the selected angle during the approach will be indicated by a displacement of the references. Correct any error smoothly and promptly with an appropriate movement of the collective lever. This method ensures a constant angle for the majority of the approach. If used in the latter stages, however, the helicopter will come to the correct hover height some distance before the intended hover point. For this reason, from about 100 ft, you must allow the landing point to move down relative to the instrument panel until it is vertically below the helicopter.

Final stages of the constant-angle approach.

Controlling the Approach Speed

Regardless of the airspeed at the start of the approach, there must be zero ground speed at the end. It follows, therefore, that during the approach, ground speed should be assessed, not airspeed. The only real way of judging whether the ground speed is correct is to scan the ground to the side of the helicopter and relate the ground speed to the distance to the hover point – i.e. the rate of closure. An apparent fast walking pace will give the correct ground speed.

The Full Approach Sequence

The level run in to the descent point should be long enough to allow you to correct any drift and ensure that the approach track is into wind. At the descent point, reduce power with the collective lever and throttle to start the descent. Once the helicopter has started to lose height, begin to reduce ground speed as required. Remember that any speed changes will require power adjustments to maintain the approach angle. During the final part of the approach, concentrate on selecting the hover attitude and allow the helicopter to drift to a stop over the landing point.

The Overshoot

If there is ever any doubt in your mind that you may not be able to maintain a safe approach, you must overshoot without hesitation. There are two main areas of misjudgement that could prove hazardous if the approach were continued:

Excessive ground speed in the latter stages In this situation, you would be faced with a rapid transition to the hover, which probably would be beyond your capability at this stage.

Excessive rate of descent with low airspeed Although ground speed is the main preoccupation, airspeed cannot be totally ignored, for if the airspeed is too low and the rate of descent high, there is a possibility that the helicopter could enter a state of vortex ring as you apply power. It is difficult to give precise figures, but in general, rates of descent in excess of 500 ft/min must be avoided at airspeeds below 17–22 kt (20–25 mph). Monitor airspeed and rate of descent during the approach; if the rate of descent exceeds 500 ft/min as the airspeed reduces through 26 kt (30 mph), you must overshoot.

Overshoot Action

To carry out an overshoot, select an accelerative attitude and, provided airspeed is above 22 kt (25 mph), apply power to climb away. Maintain a good lookout and check engine instruments in the climb.

Airmanship

- Maintain a good lookout.
- Monitor engine instruments and fuel remaining.
- Monitor wind velocity.
- Consider the significance of the avoid areas of the height/velocity graph.

CIRCUITS

The standard training circuit combines most of the skills learnt in the previous exercises. Again, lookout is extremely important, for not only will there be other aircraft in the circuit, but also aircraft joining the circuit. It is important that you do not let the need for accuracy result in a poor lookout. The purpose of this exercise is to take off to the hover, fly a standard training circuit, return to a pre-selected hover point and land.

An example of a training circuit is shown overleaf. Although it is self-explanatory, a few points need amplifying.

The climb At 400 ft on the climb out, you must carry out a climbing turn on to the crosswind leg.

The crosswind leg Roll out on the crosswind heading, correcting for drift as necessary. Continue to climb to circuit height. Use the compass and ground markers to fly accurately. The turn on to the downwind leg is made when the landing point is 45 degrees astern of the helicopter.

The downwind leg After rolling out from the turn, offset any drift to ensure that you are tracking parallel to the runway. Again, use the compass and ground markers to help you fly accurately. Complete the downwind checks as early as convenient. When the landing point is 45 degrees astern of the helicopter, carry out a speed reducing descending turn on to the base leg.

The base leg Normally, the speed will have reduced to 52 kt (60 mph) at about the same time that the helicopter is rolled out on to the base leg heading, corrected for drift. Continue descending to 400 ft and level off. Turn on to final approach.

Final approach You should be lined up with your landing point. Look for the 'sight picture' for the constant angle of approach.

Simulated Emergencies in the Circuit

As it won't be long before you will be flying your first solo on this exercise, you must be competent in handling any emergency that could occur.

Fanstops
The purpose of the fanstop is to give you practice in manoeuvring the helicopter in autorotation to a position from which a successful engine-off landing (EOL) could be made. Ideally, this position would be into wind at 300 ft above the ground, at 52 kt (60 mph) and with the helicopter level. This puts you in the

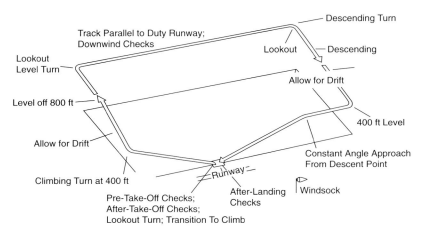

Descending Turn

Track Parallel to Duty Runway;
Downwind Checks

Lookout

Descending

Lookout
Level Turn

Allow for Drift

Level off 800 ft

400 ft Level

Allow for Drift

Constant Angle Approach
From Descent Point

Climbing Turn at 400 ft

Runway

Pre-Take-Off Checks;
After-Take-Off Checks;
Lookout Turn; Transition To Climb

After-Landing
Checks

Windsock

The circuit.

familiar position from which you will have seen and carried out variable-flare, engine-off landings. Clearly, the success of the landing would also depend on the landing surface. To this end, fly the circuit over open ground whenever possible. This applies especially to the climb out and approach paths, where the time available following a fanstop can be very limited.

Prior to carrying out a fanstop, your instructor will make an advisory call to ATC, e.g. 'G-ABCD, fanstop downwind.' You should respond to that by lowering the lever and entering autorotation. Select a field and manoeuvre toward it. When you start to carry out the re-engagement and climb away, a further radio call would be transmitted: 'G-ABCD, climbing away.'

The main consideration in a fanstop emergency is to turn the helicopter toward the most open area and, ideally, into wind. This may not be possible, however, so some compromise may be required. During the practice fanstop, if possible, simulate carrying out emergency drills and transmitting a brief mayday call. However, never allow these to distract you from the primary task.

Fanstop in the Climb
This is usually practised above 400 ft. There is time to lower the collective lever fully, but very little room for manoeuvre – no more that about 30 degrees either side of the climb heading – before being faced with the landing.

Fanstop Crosswind
Enter autorotation and turn into wind. There should be a reasonable time to manoeuvre before landing.

Fanstop Downwind
As you enter autorotation, start a turn into wind, using fairly steep angles of bank. Make sure you have 'wings level' by 300 ft regardless of the heading. In winds of less than 5 kt (6 mph), it is probably better to ignore the wind and avoid the need for a 180-degree turn.

Fanstop on Base Leg or Final Approach
As the height reduces, the room for manoeuvre reduces correspondingly.

The Hover EOL and the 180-degree EOL
Before you go solo, you will be shown a hover EOL and a 180-degree EOL by your instructor.

Airmanship

- Maintain a good lookout, especially before turning.
- Monitor engine instruments and fuel quantity.
- Monitor the wind velocity.
- Conform to ATC and R/T procedures in the circuit.
- Carry out downwind checks.

FIRST SOLO FLIGHT

The first solo flight is always an important and exciting occasion in any pilot's training. It is important because you will have demonstrated your ability to control the helicopter completely and deal with any possible emergencies.

When satisfied that you are ready to fly the helicopter solo, your instructor will brief you on exactly what to do. Normally, this takes place on the airfield before the instructor leaves the helicopter. You will be briefed to take off, fly a normal circuit and land back at the take-off point.

If you feel an approach is uncomfortable or incorrect, abandon it. The decision to carry out a go-around should be positive and made as soon as possible. Having taken the decision, carry it out without hesitation.

When flying solo, fly only as instructed; do not be tempted to deviate from the briefing. Experimenting with insufficient knowledge or technique can be fatal.

SIDEWAYS AND BACKWARD FLIGHT

This exercise is an extension of hovering, and all the same points of airmanship apply. Normally, sideways and backward flight are restricted to short distances only, or for precise positioning in the hover.

Sideways Flight

The purpose of this exercise is to fly sideways from the hover, then re-establish the hover.

Before starting to move sideways, ensure that the area is clear by carrying out a lookout turn. Select two points of reference in a line in the direction you want to travel. Keeping the reference points in line throughout the manoeuvre will help you maintain the proper ground track.

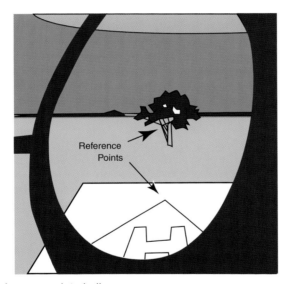

Select two reference points in line.

From a steady hover facing into wind, apply cyclic stick pressure in the desired direction of travel. As the helicopter starts to move, prevent any height loss with power and maintain the heading with the pedals. The speed of movement over the ground should be restricted to a slow walking pace for two reasons:

- There is no requirement to travel sideways at a fast speed. If the distance to be covered is great, it is far better to turn the helicopter and hover taxi.
- In the event of an engine failure at a speed above a slow walking pace, it is unlikely that the lateral movement could be stopped before the helicopter struck the ground.

Throughout the sideways movement, maintain your lookout while scanning between your attitude references ahead of the helicopter and your lateral markers. When you wish to stop, re-select the hover attitude and re-establish the hover in the normal manner.

Control Limits
As the helicopter moves sideways, it will tend to yaw in the direction of movement due to the weathercock effect. The higher the sideways speed, the greater will be the tendency to yaw. If the movement is to the right, extra left pedal will be required; ultimately, a speed will be reached where no more left pedal travel is available to prevent the yaw. The same applies to movement to the left.

For this reason, helicopter manufacturers publish sideways speed limits in their flight manuals. These limitations have a much greater application when flying sideways into wind.

Backward Flight
The purpose of this exercise is to manoeuvre backward from the hover, then re-establish the hover.

Although speed, height and heading should be controlled in the same manner as for sideways flight, manoeuvring backward poses different problems:

Lookout The obvious problem when moving backward is that you cannot see where you are going. The lookout turn will only be valid for a certain distance and time. You must restrict flying 'blind' to no more than a few yards. This will mean stopping frequently to re-check the area behind before continuing.

Hover height For backward flight, the hover height should be increased to 10 ft. This will provide greater clearance between the tail and the ground when in an increased tail-down attitude.

Heading control Select markers ahead of the helicopter to enable you to maintain the required ground track. There should be few problems with yaw control as long as the speed remains positive.

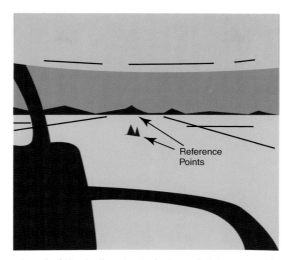

Select markers ahead of the helicopter to help maintain ground track.

Ground speed Move backward at a very slow walking pace. In fact, when headed into wind, the manoeuvre becomes more of a downwind drift in the hover.

Excessive Speed
The dangers of excessive backward speed will be demonstrated to you by your instructor. The maximum permitted backward speed is usually around 17–22 kt (20–25 mph). The main problems with flying with a negative airspeed are:

Yaw control Under negative speed conditions, the fuselage continually attempts to weathercock and turn in the direction of travel. This makes yaw control sensitive, so care must be taken to avoid over-controlling.

Attitude control Under negative airspeed conditions, attitude control produces two distinct problems:

1. **Nose-down pitch during backward flight** As the negative airspeed increases, progressively more aft cyclic stick is required to maintain helicopter attitude. A point could be reached where there is insufficient aft cyclic available to prevent the helicopter from pitching nose-down.
2. **Nose-down pitch when stopping backward flight** To stop the helicopter, the cyclic stick must be moved forward. This will cause the nose to pitch down. The helicopter will not stop immediately, however, and will continue to experience negative airspeed, which will lead to more pitching down. This final nose-down pitch, which can be very noticeable, will

depend on the airspeed and the amount by which the cyclic stick was moved initially. Even at very slow negative airspeeds with gentle cyclic movements, the effect can be very marked.

To gain proficiency in sideways and backward flying, a training square is used to practice controlling the helicopter. The exercise is started by hovering over one corner of the square, headed into wind. The the pilot flies sideways to the next corner, maintaining the into-wind heading. At each corner, the helicopter is stopped before proceeding along the next side. A landing and take-off at each corner could be included for additional practice.

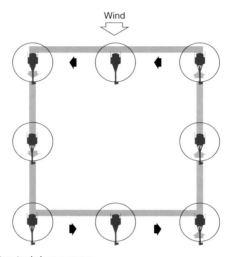

Use of the helicopter training square.

SPOT TURNS

Spot turns are manoeuvres performed at hover height, the helicopter being turned through 360 degrees, left or right, while maintaining a constant ground position. This exercise requires a high level of co-ordination with all the flight controls. When combined with sideways and backward flight, spot turns will give you complete freedom of movement when operating in the ground cushion.

Carrying Out a Spot Turn

The purpose of this exercise is to turn the helicopter through 360 degrees about the pilot position.

The pedals are used to initiate and control the rate of turn. In nil wind conditions, this poses no problems – if the initial pedal application to start the turn is maintained, it will produce an almost constant rate of turn through 360 degrees. Throughout the turn, ground position is controlled with the cyclic stick, and height with the collective lever.

When carrying out a spot turn in wind conditions, you will experience the problem of a constantly changing wind direction. This means that once pedal is applied to start the turn, maintaining that pedal position will produce varying rates of turn due to the weathercock effect. Therefore, you must look as far ahead as possible for reference, and use the pedals to maintain a constant rate of turn. During the turn, the cyclic stick will have to be offset into wind to prevent the helicopter from drifting downwind.

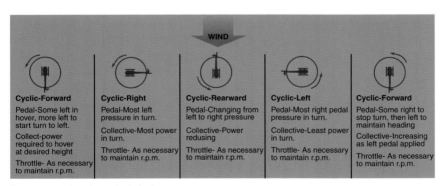

Compensating for wind during a spot turn.

In a turn to the left, more power will be required, because left pedal pressure increases the pitch angle on the tail rotor, which, in turn, requires more power from the engine. As the turn begins, the cyclic stick should be moved as necessary to keep the helicopter over the ground position. More pedal pressure will be required as the helicopter reaches the crosswind position. This is because the wind will be striking the fuselage and making it more difficult for the tail to turn into the wind. As the pedal pressure increases due to crosswind forces, you must increase the cyclic stick pressure into wind to maintain ground position. Use collective lever and throttle to maintain a constant height and engine rpm.

After 90 degrees of turn, you will need to decrease pedal pressure slightly to maintain the same rate of turn. Approaching the 180-degree position (downwind), you will need to anticipate opposite pedal pressure due to the tail moving from an upwind position to a downwind position. At this point, the rate of turn tends to increase quickly due to the weathercocking effect of the tail surfaces. Because of the tailwind condition, you will need to hold rearward cyclic stick pressure to keep the helicopter over the same spot.

Because of the helicopter's tendency to weathercock, maintaining a constant rate of turn from the 180-degree position actually requires some pedal pressure opposite to the direction of the turn. If you do not apply opposite pedal pressure, the helicopter will turn at a faster rate. The amount of pedal and cyclic stick pressure required during the turn depends on the wind velocity. As you finish the turn back into wind, apply opposite pedal pressure to stop the turn and forward cyclic pressure to prevent drifting.

Control pressures and direction of application change throughout the turn. The most dramatic change is the pedal pressure necessary to control the rate of turn as the helicopter moves through the downwind position of the turn.

Spot turns can be made in either direction. In high wind conditions, the tail rotor may not be able to produce enough thrust, which means you will not be able to control a spot turn to the right. Therefore, you should get into a habit of making the first turn of the day, or any turn after a significant weight change, to the left to check on left pedal availability. If sufficient tail rotor thrust exists to turn the helicopter through the crosswind position in a left turn, then a right turn can be accomplished successfully.

Common Errors

- Failing to maintain a constant rate of turn.
- Failing to maintain a constant ground position.
- Failing to control height and engine rpm.
- Over-controlling on the pedals.

Airmanship

- Maintain a good lookout.
- Monitor engine instruments and fuel contents.
- Monitor wind velocity, particularly in respect of the maximum wind limitations.

174

VORTEX RING RECOVERY

Vortex ring describes an aerodynamic condition where the helicopter descends vertically at a very high rate, even though power is being used.

For a helicopter to enter a vortex ring state, three conditions are required:

- An induced airflow down through the main rotor disc (powered flight).
- An upward flow of air toward the rotor disc from below, opposing the induced flow (high rate of descent).
- Low or zero airspeed.

Situations conducive to a vortex ring condition include:

- Attempting to hover OGE and not maintaining good height control.
- Recoveries from autorotation and quick stops.
- Downwind and steep powered approaches.

For vortex ring demonstrations and training in recognizing vortex ring conditions, all manoeuvres should be performed at a minimum entry height of 2,000 ft.

Entry Into Vortex Ring

From straight and level flight, reduce power to below that required to hover. Once the helicopter has settled in the descent, apply aft pressure on the cyclic stick until the airspeed approaches 17–22 kt (20–25 mph). Then allow the sink rate to increase by adjusting the attitude to obtain an airspeed of less than 9–13 kt (10–15 mph). As you approach the vortex ring state, any or all of the following symptoms may occur:

- Airframe judder.
- Random yawing, pitching and rolling.
- Variation in rpm.
- Increasing rate of descent.

Recovery From Vortex Ring

The correct recovery technique must be used, otherwise the condition will become worse. Normal pilot reaction is to increase collective pitch and add power. This response only aggravates the situation. Instead, the helicopter must be removed from the condition by increasing forward speed and/or reducing collective pitch.

When the airspeed exceeds 22 kt (25 mph), and only then, increase power to climb settings. The recovery is complete when the helicopter has passed through effective translational lift and a normal climb has been established.

Vortex ring can be avoided by selecting approach angles that are shallower than 30 degrees. When making steeper approaches, enough forward speed should be maintained to prevent the main rotor system from ingesting its own downwash.

Making your approach into wind is also an important factor in preventing this aerodynamic phenomenon.

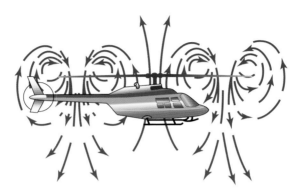

Vortex ring condition.

ENGINE-OFF LANDINGS

If the engine fails, or an emergency arises that necessitates an engine shut-down, it is essential that you have the ability to land the helicopter safely. This excercise not only will teach you the various techniques involved, but also will develop your confidence.

The different types of engine-off landings (EOLs) will be introduced to you in stages during your training. EOLs are practised on the airfield using a designated area. As an EOL is a 'committed' manoeuvre, you must ensure that your lookout is particularly good when turning on to final approach and when entering autorotation.

All EOLs, with the exception of the hover EOL, utilize either the variable-flare or constant-attitude technique. The variable flare has two distinct advantages, in that the run-on speed is lower and the collective lever is more effective. This is the technique you would normally choose if you were faced with a real engine failure. The techniques differ only in the final stages, and the main points described for the variable-flare circuit and autorotation will also apply to the constant-attitude circuit and autorotation. Pre-landing checks should be carried out before every EOL.

The EOL Circuit

This is a modification of the standard training circuit, being much smaller and flown closer to the airfield. After take-off, the climbing turn on to the crosswind leg is continued around to the downwind leg. At the end of the downwind leg, a turn is made on to final approach, maintaining height and speed. When on final approach, check the wind speed and that the landing area is clear.

Variable-Flare EOL

Give a verbal warning and enter autorotation. During the descent, carefully monitor and maintain the airspeed. As the helicopter must be straight at touch-down, i.e. the skids pointing in the direction of movement, it is important that you fly the autorotation with no drift.

The variable-flare technique can be divided into four stages:

The flare At approximately 100 ft, judged visually, apply rearward pressure on the cyclic stick to reduce ground speed progressively, aiming for a minimum of 10 kt (12 mph) at touch-down. The degree of flare will depend on the prevailing conditions. It is important that you increase the flare progressively, rather than apply too much initially and then try to reduce it later. During the flare, the helicopter must be kept straight. As well as reducing the ground speed, the flare also slows the rate of descent and causes the rotor rpm to rise. The increase in rotor rpm will make the collective lever more efficient during the cushioning of the touch-down.

Check up with collective lever When the flare starts to lose its effect on the rate of descent – at about 20–25 ft (judged visually) – make a small, but positive, check up on the collective lever. This will partially arrest the descent rate and further reduce the ground speed.

Level off Immediately after the check up on the collective lever, you must begin to reduce the flare to level the helicopter ready for the touch-down. Look well ahead and make sure the skids are pointing straight ahead.

Touch-down At this point, the helicopter will be about 4–6 ft above the ground, level and without drift. As the helicopter sinks, cushion the touch-down by raising the collective lever as much as is necessary. At the same time, you will have to apply pedal pressure to keep the helicopter straight, and cyclic pressure to prevent any tendency for the nose to pitch up. Throughout this entire phase, you should be concentrating on looking well ahead to fly the helicopter accurately. At the point of touch-down, it is imperative that the helicopter is straight, and it must be kept straight during the run-on. While the helicopter is running on, maintain the collective lever position. After the helicopter has stopped, lower the collective fully and centralize the controls.

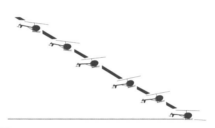

The variable-flare EOL.

Common Faults in Variable-flare EOLs
Assuming that the autorotation has been flown correctly, there are three main errors of judgement that can occur in the latter stages of a variable-flare EOL:

Insufficient flare In this case, you are faced with a high run-on speed. Do not increase the flare if you are too low, as you will run the risk of striking the ground with the tail. Level the helicopter at the normal height, accept the high speed and cushion the touch-down as usual. With the higher speed, the helicopter will tend to pitch and roll about its skids more than normal, and you must maintain the cyclic stick position. As the rotor rpm reduces, the weight will transfer to the skids, and the helicopter will slow down and stop.

Too much flare This can be caused by starting the flare too high or by flaring too hard. The net result in both cases is that the ground speed reduces too quickly. Even if the helicopter is too high, you must select the level attitude at the correct ground speed. This will mean that the bonus effects of the flare will be reduced by the time you need to cushion the touch-down. Consequently, the collective lever will be less effective.

Too much collective lever If, in cushioning the touch-down, you use the collective too early – or too much at the correct height – the helicopter will level off or even climb. The correct action is to hold the collective steady. NEVER lower it. As the rotor rpm reduces, the helicopter will start to sink once more. The overall result is that there will be less collective lever available to cushion the touch-down,

Constant-Attitude EOL

As the name suggests, you do not flare the helicopter at all during this type of EOL. The landing can be divided into two phases: the check and the touch-down. If you were to suffer an engine failure at night or in cloud, you may not see the ground in sufficient time to carry out a variable-flare EOL. By using the constant-angle technique, you should be able to carry out an EOL, even if you do not see the ground until you are within 50 ft or so. This technique can also be used in good visibility if you have had to reduce your autorotative speed to make your chosen landing point. The disadvantages of the constant-attitude technique are that both rate of descent and run-on speed are higher.

Autorotation
The autorotative airspeed should be reduced to 35 kt (40 mph). In strong winds, however, this will have to be increased to ensure that you maintain a positive ground speed. Windshear has a greater effect, and you must correct any airspeed reduction immediately. If you are below 200 ft, you should maintain the helicopter's attitude and not attempt to recover the speed.

Landing
At this point, the helicopter should be approaching the ground with skids level, no drift and a ground speed between 9 and 26 kt (10 and 30 mph), depending on the wind strength. There will be a high rate of descent. In light wind conditions, the high run-on speed has to be accepted.

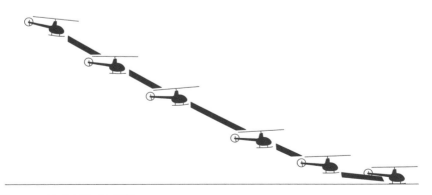

The constant-attitude EOL.

Factors Affecting EOL Performance

All-up weight At high all-up weights, the initial rate of descent will be higher and will not be offset completely by the increased rotor rpm. Therefore, the collective lever will be less effective.

Density altitude At high density altitudes, the overall effect is similar to that of high all-up weight.

Airspeed at touch-down With a reduced airspeed, the rate of descent increases as rotor rpm decreases. Therefore, reduced airspeed at touch-down reduces collective lever effectiveness.

ADVANCED AUTOROTATIONS

This exercise is an amplification of basic autorotations. It covers the techniques of adjusting speed, rotor rpm and flight path to vary the distance covered over the ground. The practical applications of this exercise will be used in practising forced landings.

At the beginning of this exercise, a normal autorotation will be carried out to provide a datum for the variations to follow. This autorotation is begun when passing over a selected ground reference point, and the distance covered by the helicopter when it passes through 400 ft is noted. Then the performance during the other autorotations is compared to this datum. When your instructor is demonstrating the various techniques, you should note the relative distances covered.

HASEL checks should be carried out before attempting a series of autorotations. Although it is not necessary to repeat all the checks each time, you should always carry out a careful lookout, especially below, before each autorotation.

Datum Autorotation

After carrying out the HASEL checks, your instructor will position the helicopter over a suitable area into wind. Then you will give a verbal warning when you can relate the helicopter's position to a reference point on the ground. Your instructor will establish a normal autorotation, whereupon you should note the rate and angle of descent. As the helicopter passes through 400 ft, make a note of a reference point on the ground. Your instructor will carry out an overshoot and reposition the helicopter for a *range autorotation*.

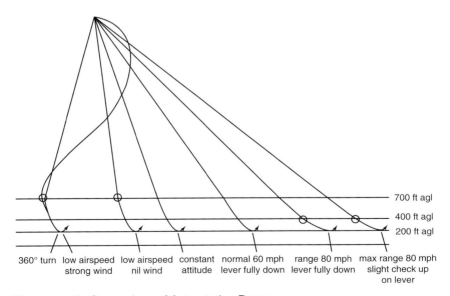

Diagrammatic Comparison of Autorotative Range.

181

Range Autorotation

Range in autorotation is a function of ground speed and rate of descent. Increasing the airspeed above 52 kt (60 mph) produces not only an increase in ground speed, but also an increase in rate of descent. The best airspeed/rate of descent combination is called the *range speed*. A further range increase can be achieved by reducing the rate of descent. Raising the collective lever to reduce rotor rpm to an optimum figure will produce the maximum range.

From straight and level flight, at the same height and entry point as for the datum autorotation, enter autorotation, but maintain 70 kt (80 mph). You will notice that although the rate of descent is higher, the descent angle is shallower. The distance covered to the 400 ft point will also be slightly greater. At 400 ft, the speed must be reduced to 52 kt (60 mph) for the overshoot. During the flare, control any tendency for the rotor rpm to increase. You will notice that there is a considerable 'float' in the flare, which increases the range even further. Maintain a good lookout and establish a normal climb.

Maximum-Range Autorotation

This is similar to the range autorotation, except that once you have settled in autorotation, you gently raise the collective lever to reduce rotor rpm toward the bottom of its limits. This will have the effect of reducing the rate of descent and descent angle, and increasing range further. Converting back to normal autorotation at 400 ft is similar to range autorotation, but in this case, the collective lever must be lowered fully to recover rotor rpm. Both control movements should be smooth and co-ordinated so that there is no sudden change in the flight path.

Constant-Attitude Autorotation

As well as reducing range, the constant-attitude autorotation provides the basis for an EOL whenever the variable-flare type is either impractical or inadvisable. This may be due to low speed or height at the time of entry, a situation when a variable-flare type might be difficult to judge (e.g. at night) or a late speed reduction during a forced landing. The minimum speed of 30–35 kt (35–40 mph) is a compromise between having as low a forward speed as possible and avoiding very high rates of descent, which would cause problems for landing.

From straight and level flight, using the same height and entry point as before, enter autorotation and reduce speed to 30 kt (35 mph). The rate of descent will be higher than normal, and the descent angle much steeper. (In strong winds, it can be almost vertical.) Because the airspeed will be lower than that in the datum autorotation, the rotor rpm will also be lower. It is important to monitor the airspeed closely during the descent – even a reduction of a few knots will increase the rate of descent substantially. The greatest risk of losing airspeed occurs below 500 ft, because wind shear becomes more apparent.

At 400 ft, the distance covered will be much less than the 52 kt (60 mph) autorotation. During the recovery, there will be a greater tendency for the nose to pitch up as power is increased. Quite large cyclic stick movements will be required to maintain attitude. Any significant loss of airspeed during the recovery could cause the helicopter to enter vortex ring conditions. When you have completed the recovery, establish a normal climb and maintain a good lookout.

Low-Speed Autorotation

The low-speed autorotation reduces range to a minimum. For it to be most effective, the airspeed must be reduced as quickly as possible after entry. In very light wind conditions, there will always be some ground speed, but in stronger winds, it is possible to achieve a negative ground speed.

From straight and level flight, using the same height and entry point as before, enter autorotation and reduce speed by applying rearward cyclic pressure to give a nose-up attitude (15 degrees). As the airspeed falls to the lowest positive mark on the ASI, adjust the attitude to maintain this speed – this may mean that the helicopter is moving backward over the ground. Note the very high rate of descent.

To recover safely from this type of autorotation, first you must re-establish a normal 52 kt (60 mph) autorotation. Note that the distance covered at the 400 ft point is less than the constant-attitude autorotation. The overshoot is as normal.

Remember always that, in autorotation, it is far easier to lose distance over the ground than to regain it.

Turns in Autorotation

The low-speed autorotation is a satisfactory method of descending to a position vertically below the helicopter only when the wind is strong. In light winds, the best way of achieving this is to carry out a 360-degree turn if height permits. If the wind is strong, a turn through 360 degrees at 30 degrees of bank would result in the helicopter being blown downwind. In this situation, the helicopter may finish up short of the intended touch-down point.

Using the same entry point and height, establish a normal autorotation at 52 kt (60 mph) and roll into a 30-degree turn. This angle is a compromise between a fast rate of turn and a low rate of descent. During the turn, ensure that both airspeed and angle of bank are maintained. Control rpm as necessary. As you roll out heading into wind, note the overall height loss. Normally, this will be in the order of 1,200–1,500 ft. The helicopter must be level for the overshoot at 400 ft, even if the turn is not complete. The overshoot is as normal.

Airmanship

- Carry out HASEL checks before a series of autorotations.
- Maintain a lookout, especially before low-speed autorotations and during turns.
- Terminate autorotations into wind.
- Be aware of rotor rpm limits for autorotation.
- Remember the verbal warning.
- Remember the dangers of vortex ring and the conditions that could induce it.

FORCED LANDINGS

This exercise is the practical application of the techniques learnt in the previous lesson. You will be taught various techniques that will enable you to manoeuvre from the point of entering autorotation to a position where you can carry out a safe EOL into a suitable area.

When practising forced landings, do not be tempted to carry on below the minimum authorized overshoot height.

Initially, while you are learning the techniques, there will be no element of surprise. Later on, the emergency will be called by the words, 'Practice engine failure – Go!' You must act quickly to enter autorotation smoothly and start to look for a suitable landing area. If it is not immediately obvious that you need to go for a range or low-speed autorotation, you should establish a normal autorotation at 52 kt (60 mph) to give you the minimum rate of descent and maximum time in the air.

Selecting a Suitable Landing Area

In autorotation, the overall range of the helicopter will depend on the airspeed, height above the ground and wind velocity at the time of entry. To give yourself the widest possible choice of landing area, never fly lower than is necessary. In the case of a real engine failure, a rapid assessment of conditions and selection of a landing area must be made. In view of this, always keep in mind the wind velocity and possible landing areas whenever you are flying.

During this exercise, your instructor will point out possible forced landing areas and discuss their suitability under the prevailing wind conditions. As the wind strength increases, it will have a greater influence on the choice of landing direction. In light winds, you will be able to accept a greater out-of-wind component during landing than in moderate winds. As the wind becomes stronger, it will become the predominant factor in choosing your landing direction.

When selecting a suitable landing area, you need to consider the following factors (the five 'Ss'):

Size Always try to select the largest space available.

Shape With an irregularly-shaped area, relate the direction with the longest clear run-on to the prevailing wind.

Surrounds If your selected landing area has other good areas adjacent to it, they may give you useful options during the forced landing.

Surface Avoid rough uneven surfaces, marshy areas and fields with tall standing crops. If you are forced to land in a ploughed field, do so along the line of the furrows.

Slope If possible, select a level area to land on. Slope can be difficult to judge from height – beware!

Having selected the landing area and direction, you must choose an aiming point. The forced landing pattern will be flown with this in mind. Normally, you should aim for a point about a third of the distance into the area.

There are many ways in which a forced landing pattern can be flown to set up an EOL into the selected area. How successfully you employ any, or all, of the techniques previously learnt will depend largely on your ability to visualize the flight path into the selected area.

In the lesson on advanced autorotations, you will have flown various techniques and noted the distances covered. Now you must aim to adjust airspeed to reach a specific point on the ground. If you are established in autorotation at the correct speed to reach your aiming point, that point will remain in a constant position in the windshield. If the point starts to move up the windshield, you are undershooting, and you should increase speed until the point remains static in the windshield again. If the point starts to move down the windshield, you are overshooting, and you should reduce speed until the point remains static in the windshield again. Initially, the airspeed figure itself is immaterial, although it must remain positive. It only becomes important when you need to convert it to a speed from which you can carry out an EOL. If your speed is much above 52 kt (60 mph), you must allow for considerable float as you reduce speed to 52 kt (60 mph) for the variable-flare EOL.

S-Turns in Autorotation

You can use S-turns whenever you need to lose height without covering too much distance. This situation can occur when you are high on the final approach, not high enough to do a 360-degree turn, and the wind is so light that a low-speed technique would carry you too far forward. S-turns should be carried out at 48–52 kt (55–60 mph), and you should NEVER turn more than 90 degrees away from your touch-down heading. You should reduce the size of the S-turns as your height decreases. Again, always ensure that you are level laterally by 300 ft at the latest.

The Forced Landing Pattern

You can use any combination of all the techniques you have learnt to construct your forced landing pattern. The choice of whether to employ large turns or low-speed techniques will depend largely upon the height available and the wind speed. Strong winds favour low-speed autorotations, whereas in light winds, turns are preferable. When formulating your plan, you may wish to consider these broad guidelines:

- Once autorotation is established, select a suitable area and turn toward it.
- Manoeuvre until you are close to the area and stay there.
- Always allow plenty of height for any turns.

186

Ideally, every forced landing should terminate with a variable-flare EOL, rather than a constant-attitude EOL. This is because the rate of descent will be lower, and the touch-down speed will be slower.

Vital Actions

Virtually all your concentration and effort during a forced landing should be devoted to flying the helicopter. Only when that aim is being achieved should you think about carrying out the appropriate emergency drills (vital actions). Memorize the relevant drills and try to transmit a brief mayday call if time permits. Remember to keep an eye on your intended landing area between carrying out the vital actions, adjusting the autorotative approach if necessary. Ideally, you should carry out the complete set of checks, but again, your prime responsibility is to fly the helicopter to a position from which a safe EOL can be carried out.

A typical vital-action check-list would include the following:

- Mayday call.
- Mixture control to idle cut-off.
- Magneto switches off.
- Generator off.
- Fuel valve off.
- All harnesses locked and tight.
- Battery switch off when finished with radio.

PRECISION TRANSITIONS

Helicopter manoeuvres are rarely rushed and, as a general policy, abrupt changes in attitude should be avoided if at all possible. There are circumstances, however, when a rapid deceleration is imperative. For example, a helicopter operating in reduced visibility may have to stop quickly to avoid obstructions. The technique for this is called a *quick stop*, and it will be the subject of the lesson following this.

Precision transitions provide an intermediate training step to quick stops. They require very little flare and, as a result, deceleration is much slower. The purpose of the exercise is to develop control co-ordination and confidence by moving from one point to another across the airfield while maintaining a constant height, heading and engine speed.

Normally, they are practised into wind. Carrying out this exercise downwind should be avoided, especially in strong winds, as the complete loss of translational lift while drifting out of ground effect could be hazardous to say the least. As this exercise involves utilizing a large part of the airfield, it is important that you maintain a good lookout at all times.

Air Exercise

The transition is started from a steady hover facing into wind. First select a 'keep straight' marker as far ahead as possible. Carry out a lookout turn to make sure the approach is clear. Gently apply forward pressure to the cyclic stick to start the transition forward. As the helicopter leaves the ground cushion, it will want to sink. This must be prevented by a small amount of power – keep straight with the pedals – and as the speed increases further, more forward cyclic stick pressure will be required to overcome flapback. At this point, translational lift will be felt, and the helicopter will want to climb.

This must be prevented by reducing power as necessary to maintain height. Pedal pressure will be required to maintain the heading.

After reaching 30–35 kt (35–40 mph), you have to begin the decelerative process to return to the hover. Start the deceleration by applying rearward pressure on the cyclic stick, and counteract any climbing tendency with power. Keep straight with pedal. As the helicopter gradually slows down and loses the effects of translational lift, apply power to maintain a constant height. Again, pedal control is necessary to maintain the heading.

The final part of the transition is quite difficult to co-ordinate unless you take your time. The main rotor disc must be placed in the hover attitude at just the right time to bring the helicopter back into the hover and arrest the ground speed.

All of these effects place a heavy demand on the collective lever and throttle. These controls must be applied smoothly to maintain a constant height. Similarly, the pedals may call for a considerable movement in re-establishing the hover.

The precision transition.

Airmanship

- Perform a lookout turn before every precision transition.
- Monitor wind velocity.
- Monitor engine instruments and fuel quantity.
- Avoid over-controlling the flare and possible tail strikes at low heights.
- Select heading references.

QUICK STOPS

Essentially, quick stops are advanced co-ordination exercises, but they do have some operational applications whenever a rapid transition from forward flight to the hover is required. Because these are low-level manoeuvres, you must use external references almost exclusively when judging attitude, angle of bank, height and heading, making only brief checks of flight and engine instruments. Normally, this exercise is carried out on the airfield, so a good lookout is essential at all times.

Quick Stop Into Wind

Flare effects When the helicopter is flared, it will experience certain effects. These flare effects will increase in magnitude as the overall attitude change, rate of attitude change or entry speed increases. As the whole point of the quick stop is to reduce ground speed rapidly to zero, it is important to judge the flare by reference to ground speed.

Height The helicopter will want to climb as soon as it is flared.

Heading With a reduction in airspeed, the helicopter will yaw to the left.

Power The flare produces an increase in engine rpm. If height is maintained by lowering the collective lever, the throttle must be reduced to prevent an engine over-speed. Pedal should be applied as necessary to maintain the heading.

Air Exercise

Normally, the quick stop will be started from the hover, although it can be started from straight and level flight. Quick stops always finish heading into wind. The first few entries will be at low speeds so that the control movements and effects can be seen more easily. As co-ordination is acquired, the entry speed will be increased progressively. The object of the quick stop is to maintain height (30 ft), heading (into wind) and rpm until the hover is established.

The quick stop is initiated by a verbal warning: 'Quick stop, quick stop – Go!' On the word, 'Go', flare the helicopter, at the same time, lowering the collective lever at a sufficient rate to maintain height, and controlling rpm with the throttle. Apply right pedal to maintain balance. Continue to lower the lever while increasing the flare to maintain height. As the flare starts to lose its effect, raise the collective lever to increase power and maintain height. The helicopter will be decelerating rapidly; just before the ground speed reaches zero, select the hover attitude with the cyclic stick and apply power to establish the hover. Maintain heading with pedal as necessary.

Throughout the quick stop, use your heading reference marker and try to avoid over-controlling on the pedals. During the entry, the helicopter may 'fishtail' quite noticeably. During the final stages, as power is applied, you will need to anticipate the large amount of left pedal that will be needed. Once you have established a steady hover, move gently forward and down to the normal hover height.

Quick Stop Errors
There are three major errors that can occur when practising this exercise:

Flaring too low Obviously, at very low level, it would be possible to strike the tail during the flare. This is why you practise quick stops at 30 ft.

Descending in the flare Even if the flare is started at the correct height, if you allow it to sink in the flare, the tail could strike the ground. Also, if the airspeed is low and power is being applied, the conditions for vortex ring exist.

Maintaining the flare with zero ground speed If the flare is maintained with zero ground speed and power applied, the helicopter would start to move backward. This could lead to negative airspeed and possible over-controlling.

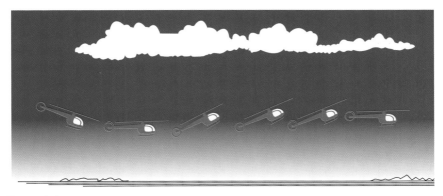

The quick stop.

Downwind Emergency Turn
The downwind emergency turn is simply a steep level turn from a downwind or crosswind position into wind.

From straight and level flight, roll smoothly into a steep turn and maintain balance with the pedals. Once in the turn, flare the helicopter and use the collective lever to control the height. The rate of turn will increase as the airspeed reduces – ensure that you maintain at least 26 kt (30 mph) until the helicopter is heading within 30 degrees of the wind. Roll out of the turn heading into wind and maintain the flare to reduce the ground speed to zero, at the same time increasing power to establish the hover in the usual way. Then move gently forward and down to the normal hover height.

PILOT NAVIGATION

Successful navigation depends on correct division of your effort between flying the helicopter, monitoring time and position at intervals, and calculating error corrections. The division of time required will vary according to flight visibility, speed and the accuracy of your planning. Take care to plan carefully, and trust your plan unless it is obviously wrong. Always look and think ahead, and do not try to read too much map detail. Use heading and times in conjunction with map features.

Pre-Flight Planning

Accurate pre-flight planning, amended in flight as necessary with simple mental calculations, will contribute greatly to the success of any flight. By careful study of the route before take-off, you will be able to form a mental picture of the intended track, which will greatly simplify the recognition of landmarks. The sense of preparedness for what lies ahead has considerable influence on successful air navigation.

Preparation of Maps
No hard and fast rules apply to the marking of maps in preparation for a flight. Obviously, a track line is necessary to provide a datum for checking the progress of the flight. Suitable intervals along the track can be indicated by any of the following:

Time scales These can be at intervals of any number of minutes based on the estimated ground speed.

Proportional division The track can be marked at quarter, half and three-quarter distance intervals, with the corresponding flight times noted alongside each mark.

Proportional division.

Distance scales Marks along the track at 5-mile intervals will provide a useful reference for estimating distances and helping with mental calculations.

Dotted lines drawn at 5 degrees on each side of track, through the start and destination points, will be helpful when considering heading alternatives.

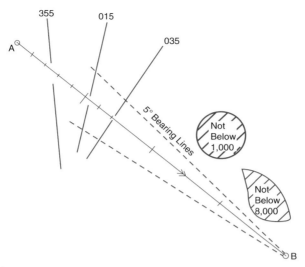

Distance scales.

Ideally, maps should be folded so that the complete track can be covered with the minimum number of page turns and the problems of re-folding in flight avoided.

Mental Deduced Reckoning Navigation (Mental DR NAV)

Sometimes, it is useful to be able to solve mentally the problems normally undertaken by the navigation computer, even though the answers may be approximate. Quick mental methods are used extensively in pilot navigation. The mental solution of problems can be conveniently dealt with under the following headings:

Estimation of Distance
Constant practice on the ground in mental estimation of distances on maps is necessary to improve accuracy. In addition, the following aids may de used :

Hand measurements The span of the hand from thumb to little finger will provide a reliable measure if its dimension is known in terms of the scale of map being used. The distance from thumbnail to knuckle crease is useful for short distances.

Parallels of latitude On a map, these provide useful visual aids measuring distance.

Estimation of Direction
As with estimation of distance, constant practice is necessary to become accurate in estimating direction. The following methods will be of assistance:

Use of 5-degree bearing lines Bearing lines are useful for the rapid estimation of errors in track by comparing fixes en route with the intended track and 5-degree bearing lines. For example, the figure below shows a pin-point locating the helicopter over B, approximately three-fifths of the distance from the planned track to a 5-degree bearing line. Therefore, the angle between actual and planned track (track error) is 3 degrees.

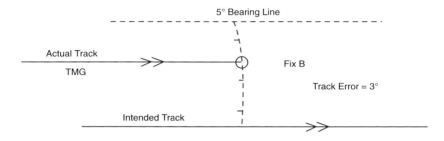

TMG = Track Made Good

Use of 5-degree bearing lines.

The 1 in 60 rule The 1 in 60 rule is a very useful method of estimating small angles. It is based on the fact that 1 naut.mile subtends an angle of 1 degree at an approximate distance of 60 naut.miles.

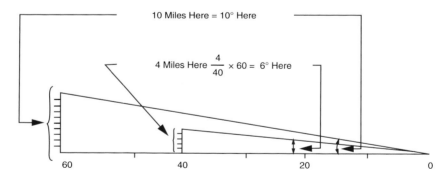

Basic Application of the One-in-Sixty Rule

The 1 in 60 rule.

Bisecting the angle Having decided in which quadrant the required track lies, the angle can be estimated quite accurately by progressively mentally halving the sector in which it lies, and finally interpolating between the estimated 'bracket lines'.

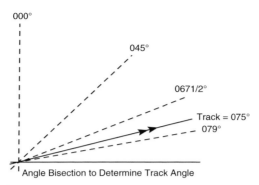

Angle Bisection to Determine Track Angle

Bisecting the angle.

Estimation of Wind Effect

On ground speed The maximum effect of wind speed is felt when the wind direction is from ahead or astern of track and decreases to approximately zero on the beam.

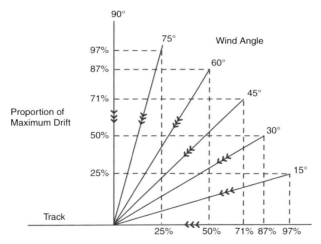

Proportion of Wind Strength Affecting Ground Speed

Estimation of wind effect.

On drift Similarly, the angle of wind to track may be expressed as a factor of the maximum possible drift resulting when the wind is on the beam. Maximum drift is determined by the 1 in 60 rule, using the wind speed and airspeed vectors. Then the maximum drift is reduced by the factor for the wind direction involved. When the drift is known, the course to steer can be calculated to make good the particular track required. These calculations are only approximate, but are acceptable in pilot navigation.

Estimation of Time of Arrival (ETA)

Sometimes, ETA can be estimated without calculating the ground speed. The two most common methods are:

Modifying flight plan times by proportion Imagine that a helicopter arrives at a checkpoint after 18 min instead of the predicted 20 min, thereby gaining 2 min in 20, or 1/10. If 50 min of flight plan time remain, the helicopter can be expected to gain a further $50 \times 1/10 = 5$ min. Thus, the helicopter will arrive 7 min ahead of the original ETA.

Estimating leg time by proportion Imagine about 2 in (50 mm) of a leg on the map have been covered in 11 min. This distance is stepped off along the remainder of the track. If the distance to go is estimated to be, say, three-and-a-third times the distance covered, the time to go will be a further 37 min.

Map Analysis

It is important that pilots familiarize themselves with the symbols and general properties of the maps they use. In map analysis, however, the process is carried one step further. Attention is given to whole areas along the intended route, assessing in detail all the various features, so that a full mental picture can be built up. A logical sequence of extracting this information is necessary, and the following is a typical example:

General location The general aspects of the area to be flown over should be considered – whether the area is coastal or inland, flat or hilly, etc. Then the route should be divided into sections, and within each section, areas having the same general characteristics should be shown.

Relief This is well portrayed by contour lines or layer tinting.

Coastline or water features The nature of a coastline is important, cliffs, sand dunes and beaches being outstanding features. Lakes are very distinctive landmarks, being recognizable by the shape, position of islands and surrounding woodland, etc. Indentations such as estuaries are excellent features for gaining fixes.

Agricultural and built-up areas Again, the general features of the area should be studied. The shapes of wooded areas will provide a valuable insight into what to expect en route. Built-up areas also form distinctive landmarks by virtue of their size and shape. Mines, brickworks, churches, cemeteries, etc. are usually indicated on the map and provide easily recognizable pin-points.

Communications Almost invariably, roads and railways lead into important focal areas, and their patterns are useful. Single and double tracks, embankments and cuttings, bridges and tunnels are all aids to identification.

Special features This covers the remaining miscellaneous features, such as airfields, radio stations, power lines, lighthouses, etc.

Map Reading

There are four basic factors upon which the success of map reading depends: knowledge of direction, knowledge of distance, identification of features and selection of landmarks.

Direction The first action in map reading is to orientate the map. By doing so, the pilot relates the direction of land features to their representations on the map, thereby aiding recognition.

Distance When the map has been orientated properly, it will be easier to compare distances between landmarks on the ground with their corresponding distances on the map, thus facilitating the fixing of position.

Anticipation of landmarks In pre-flight planning, the relationship of easily recognizable features to the intended track will have been noted and a time established at which the helicopter will be in their vicinity. Thus, in flight, the pilot will be prepared to make a visual observation at a particular time, avoiding undue diversion of attention from other aspects of the flight.

Check features and priority selection The basic principle governing the selection of best check features is the ease with which they can be identified. They must be readily distinguishable from their surroundings. The conspicuousness of any check feature depends on:

1. Angle of observation At low levels, features are more easily recognized from their outline in elevation, rather than in plan. As height is increased, the plan outline becomes more important.
2. **Uniqueness of the feature** To avoid ambiguity, the ideal feature should be the only one of its particular outline in the vicinity.
3. **Contrast and colour** These properties play a large part in the identification of a particular feature. Map reading may be complicated by seasonal variations.

Fixing by Map Reading

Map reading techniques are largely dependent upon the weather. They have been developed for:

- Conditions that permit continuous visual observation of the ground.
- Conditions that limit visual observations of the ground to unpredictable intervals.

Map Reading in Continuous Conditions
By means of a time scale on track, graduated to ground speed, the pilot can be prepared to look for a definite feature at a definite time. As a check on identification, other ground details surrounding the feature should be confirmed positively.

Thus, when in continuous contact with the ground, read from map to ground.

Map Reading at Unpredictable Intervals
This technique should be used when flying, or descending, through broken cloud. First the pilot estimates a circle of uncertainty for his position, based on a 10 per cent error of the distance flown from his last known position. A steady heading is maintained, and the circle of uncertainty moves along with the estimated DR position, increasing in diameter. The pilot studies the ground features over which the helicopter is flying, noting outstanding features and the sequence in which they occur. Then the pilot attempts to identify these features on the map within the circle of uncertainty. If identified, they allow a ground position and track made good to be established.

Thus, when seeking to establish position, read from ground to map.

Procedure When Uncertain of Position
It is not possible to specify a firm procedure to be adopted by a pilot who is uncertain of position, because the course of action required will depend on the circumstances pertaining at the time.

A pilot who has two-way radio communication should make full use of available direction finding and fixing facilities *before* it is too late for assistance to be given.

Check safety altitude and fuel quantity remaining and fly for endurance. Turn toward the nearest unique line feature. On the way to the line feature, attempt to fix the position by map reading, using the techniques described. If position is established, decide whether the destination or diversion is within range.

Airmanship
Remember that when you allocate your time between navigation and flying, you must still carry out the normal airmanship checks:

• Maintain a good lookout.
• Monitor engine and fuel instruments.
• Monitor the weather, especially the wind velocity.
• Make more frequent cross-checks with the compass.

OUT-OF-WIND MANOEUVRES

This exercise concentrates on the various techniques used in operating the helicopter out of wind. Downwind transitions are similar to those into wind, but with the additional problems of power, control and safety (avoid curve). The exercise is about learning new techniques, and no attempt will be made to introduce power limitations. Before you practice downwind exercises, however, you should ensure that you have a sufficient power margin available. Do not carry out downwind transitions in wind speeds greater than 25 kt (29 mph). As you will be operating against the normal circuit direction, you must keep a good lookout at all times.

Hovering Out of Wind

Hovering out of wind is very similar to sideways and backward flying, in that the helicopter is experiencing an airspeed. In this exercise, the four hover positions are linked by means of a lookout turn. The control positions and power settings in the out-of-wind cases are related to the into-wind hover. The degree of control position change required will depend on the wind speed.

Hover with left crosswind In this position, the cyclic stick should be offset into wind; the helicopter will hover more left skid low. Due to the weathercock effect, increased left pedal will be required, which will demand an increase in power.

Hover downwind Again, the cyclic stick should be offset into wind. From this, you might expect the attitude to be more nose-up, when in fact it will be less nose-up. This is due to the decreased effect of the downwash on the stabilizer when hovering downwind. The pedals will be quite sensitive, and care must be taken to avoid over-controlling. Prolonged hovering downwind should be avoided, due to the danger of engine fumes entering the cabin.

Hover with right crosswind The cyclic stick should be offset into wind; the helicopter will hover more level. Less left pedal will be needed, so power required will be less.

In view of the fact that hovering with a left crosswind requires the most left pedal and power, you should always confirm that a hover in that position is possible before attempting a hover in the other two positions, unless the wind is very light.

From the Hover, Manoeuvre in Any Direction and Re-Establish the Hover
Manoeuvring in this way combines the techniques associated with sideways and backward flying, and hovering out of wind. The cyclic stick should be moved in the direction of travel, while the height and heading should be controlled and maintained as normal. It is important to note that when heading

out of wind, the ground speed of the manoeuvre plus the wind speed must not exceed the limit of the helicopter type. When manoeuvring downwind, monitor ground speed carefully to avoid excessive speed.

The Parallel Heading Square

This incorporates downwind and crosswind hovering into the pattern, and can be started from any corner of the square. The helicopter is hovered over the ground track with its longitudinal axis aligned with one side of the square. As each corner is reached, the helicopter is stopped before being turned and aligned with the next side.

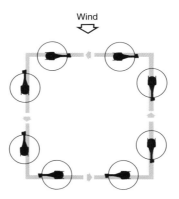

The parallel heading square.

Perpendicular Heading Square

This pattern is flown with the helicopter outside the square and its longitudinal axis perpendicular to a side. The helicopter should not be stopped at the corners, but turned in one continuous motion.

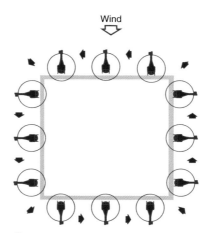

The perpendicular heading square.

Figures of Eight
These can be flown using constant, parallel or perpendicular headings, as shown in the figure below. Regardless of the method, the pattern should be flown slowly and smoothly at a constant height, without pausing until the pattern is completed.

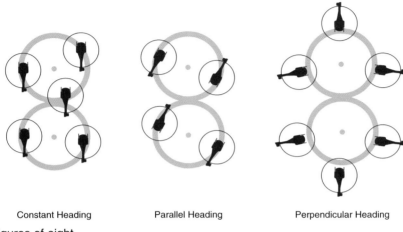

Constant Heading   Parallel Heading   Perpendicular Heading

Figures of eight.

Take-Off and Landing Out of Wind
Basically, the problems of landing and taking off out of wind are the same as those encountered when flying sideways and backward out of wind. The same limitations also apply. The maximum wind velocity for crosswind and downwind take-offs and landings is 25 kt (29 mph).

The landing is controlled as normal, but extra care must be taken to ensure that no lateral movement occurs at the point of touch-down.

Crosswind landing With a crosswind from the left, the helicopter attitude will be more left skid low, as the cyclic stick will be offset to the left. With a crosswind from the right, the attitude will be almost level, as the cyclic stick will be offset to the right. In both cases, the disc attitude should be maintained with the cyclic stick until the helicopter has settled on both skids. At this point, the cyclic stick may be centralized gradually as the collective lever is lowered to the fully-down position and power is reduced. The pedals may become quite sensitive, and care must be taken to avoid over-controlling.

Downwind landing The technique required is much the same as for the crosswind case. The pedals can be extremely sensitive, especially at high all-up weights.

Crosswind take-off Having just landed the helicopter in the crosswind position, you will have some idea of the approximate control positions required for the take-off. Pre-set these positions before raising the collective lever so that only small adjustments will be required as the helicopter lifts off. As with any take-off, you should make it a positive manoeuvre.

Downwind take-off From this position, the technique differs in that the collective lever should be raised slightly before the cyclic stick is offset into wind. Subsequently, the technique is similar to that used for crosswind take-offs. Again, try to avoid over-controlling on the pedals.

Downwind Transitions

So that you do not lightly accept a downwind transition, there are three implications that need to be considered when comparing it with the into-wind case:

Power The power margins required for the various techniques will be greater than those needed for the into-wind situation, because the helicopter must have sufficient power available to go through the zero-airspeed position. The power margins required are the same as for hover OGE performance.

Manoeuvrability The problems of power coupled with high ground speed and low airspeed will lead to reduced manoeuvrability should you need to turn the helicopter during the transition, to take avoiding action for example.

Emergencies The high ground speed/low airspeed condition places the helicopter in a poor situation should you need to abort the transition due to an emergency.

Downwind Cushion Creep Transition from the Hover
Confirm that the power margin is sufficient and carry out a lookout turn. When steady in the hover downwind again, select a heading reference marker. Initiate the transition with a gentle cyclic stick movement. Prevent any sink with power and allow the helicopter to accelerate close to the ground. Depending on the wind strength, the ground speed can be comparatively high with no indication of airspeed. At the onset of translational lift (more marked than when into wind), allow the helicopter to climb slightly, but keep it accelerating. As the ground speed will be high, the angle of climb will be shallower than into wind. If necessary, select the best angle of climb to clear any obstacles, otherwise use the normal 52 kt (60 mph) climb.

Downwind Approach to the Hover
Fly the downwind circuit and extend well upwind, as, unlike normal circuits, you will be drifted in toward your landing point during the turn on to final approach. This extension will also give you time to reduce the airspeed slightly so that you will roll out on final approach at slightly below 52 kt (60 mph).

Begin a descent for a slightly shallower than normal angle and carefully monitor both ground speed and rate of descent. Once the airspeed has reduced to 26–30 kt (30–35 mph), the rate of descent must not be greater than 500 ft/min. This point will occur much sooner in the downwind approach than in the into-wind approach. As the ground speed reduces, the airspeed will become zero and eventually negative. This change from positive to negative airspeed raises the following considerations:

Power required There will be a marked increase in power required to maintain the approach as translational lift is lost and the airspeed falls through zero. What initially may look like a large power reserve can quickly become quite small.

Vortex ring Of necessity, a large portion of the approach will be at low or negative airspeed. If the rate of descent is not monitored closely and is allowed to increase above 500 ft/min, a vortex ring condition could develop.

Heading control You will have experienced already the problems of heading control with negative airspeed. In gusty conditions, the pedals will be extra sensitive, which could cause over-controlling.

Cyclic stick In the final stages of the approach with a forward CG and a strong tailwind, the cyclic stick could reach its aft limit. If this does occur, carry out a run-on landing.

Overshooting
Any decision to overshoot must be positive and made in good time. You must overshoot if directional control becomes difficult.

Establishing the Hover Downwind
In the latter stages of the approach, you should concentrate on carrying out as gentle a transition to the hover as possible. This will be achievable only if you keep the ground speed under control. Avoid any sudden attitude changes, large power increases or over-controlling on the pedals. Because the hover is more difficult to establish than when into wind, aim for a higher hover than normal. If you need to land, turn into wind first.

Airmanship
The main points of airmanship for this exercise are:

- Maintain a good lookout – you will be operating against the normal circuit traffic.
- Monitor engine and fuel instruments.
- Monitor the wind velocity – 25 kt (29 mph) limit.

SLOPING GROUND

The art of landing and taking off from sloping ground requires gentleness and smooth control movements. Avoid any tailwind component if possible, as this will make control of landings and take-offs more difficult.

Landing From the Hover

Never land with the tail up the slope for obvious reasons, and always be aware of the wind direction, noting it as you approach the sloping ground. Carry out a visual inspection of the area using the five 'Ss' technique explained earlier:

Size If the sloping ground is in the form of a bowl rather than a mound, ensure there is sufficient room to operate within it.

Shape The shape of the area may only offer slope in certain directions. Relating these to the wind velocity will determine which slopes you will be able to land on and the direction of landing. Try to avoid landing directions that will present you with a compound slope.

Surrounds Note any obstructions on or around the sloping ground.

When you have selected the slope and landing direction, you need to manoeuvre over the slope to select the landing point. As you manoeuvre, ensure that there is a safe clearance, not only between the ground and the skids, but also between the ground and the main rotor disc. If you need to turn the helicopter, always turn the tail away from the slope. To choose a specific landing point on the slope, you need to consider the remaining two 'Ss':

Surface Some areas of the slope may have rough or worn surfaces; it is probably safer to land across a slippery surface than on an upslope heading.

Slope The degree of slope will vary from one part to another. Discount any areas that appear to have a slope outside your limits.

Refer to the figure opposite. Once established over your selected landing point in a steady hover, carry out the pre-landing checks and select a heading reference marker (1).

A landing on sloping ground can be split into three distinct phases. Using the left skid-upslope landing as an example, these are: hover to left skid in contact; left skid in contact to both skids in contact; and both skids in contact to collective lever fully down. Note, however, that with no crosswind component, the helicopter hovers left skid low, so landing with the right skid upslope will be easier than left skid upslope. The technique is the same.

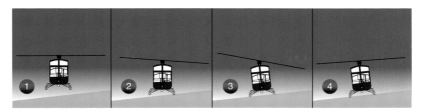

Landing on sloping ground.

Hover to Left Skid in Contact
Proceed as for a normal landing until the left skid touches the ground (2). It is most important that there be no lateral movement at this point. Once in contact, a very slight lowering of the collective lever will ensure that the skid is firmly positioned.

Left Skid in Contact to Both Skids in Contact
With only one skid on the ground, the helicopter will be sensitive to both cyclic stick and yaw pedal movements, so you must be steady on these controls. The helicopter must be pivoted about the left skid until the right skid makes contact with the ground (3). This pivoting is achieved by carefully co-ordinating the movements of the collective lever and the cyclic stick. As the collective lever is gently lowered, the cyclic stick must be moved progressively into the slope to keep the rotor disc horizontal. The rate of pivoting should be controlled until eventually, the right skid touches the ground. As with any other landing, pedal pressure must be applied to maintain heading.
Abort the landing if any of the following occur:

Mislanding If any yawing of the helicopter occurs or it begins to slide down the slope.

Insufficient rotor disc clearance On an uneven slope, it is possible that moving the cyclic stick toward the slope will place the main rotor disc too close to the ground. You must monitor this closely as you move the cyclic stick in the direction of the slope.

Reaching the cyclic stick stop Obviously, there is a physical limit to the amount of offset cyclic stick that can be applied. There may be times when sufficient cyclic stick movement is not available. Your instructor will demonstrate this limit to you during the exercise.

If you need to abort the landing, make sure that the take-off is positive, then re-establish the hover at a safe height.

Both Skids in Contact to Collective Lever Fully Down
With the right skid touching the ground, gradually lower the collective lever to increase the weight on the skids. As you do so, gradually centralize the cyclic stick and pedals (4). This final action may cause the fuselage to roll about the skids. Carry out the post-landing checks.

Landing Heading Nose Upslope
Although the overall technique of landing with the nose pointed upslope is similar to that used when landing with left or right skid upslope, there are several additional points to consider:

* There will be very little clearance between the nose of the helicopter and the slope. For this reason, a landing should be carried out near the top of the slope.
* The helicopter will make initial contact with the front of both skids. As the area of contact will be very small, heading control will be extremely sensitive.
* When pivoting the helicopter, it is not only easier to slide down the slope, but also possible to creep up the slope.
* On smooth or, worse, slippery surfaces, there is a greater possibility that the helicopter will slide down the slope as the weight is transferred to the skids.

Take-Off to the Hover
The take-off from sloping ground can be split into two phases: assume the hover attitude; and lift off to the hover. The technique for a take-off with left skid upslope is described, but it is the same for a take-off with right skid upslope. A similar method is employed for a nose-upslope take-off.

Carry out the pre-take-off checks and select a heading reference marker.

Assume the Hover Attitude
Refer to the figure opposite. Having just landed you will have some idea of the approximate positions required for the cyclic stick and pedals. As you pre-set them, check the ground clearance of the rotor disc carefully and avoid the cyclic stops (1). Gently raise the collective lever, anticipating yaw with pedal. As you raise the collective lever progressively, use the cyclic stick to keep the disc level. In this way, the helicopter will pivot about the left skid until it is in the hover attitude (2).

Taking off from sloping ground.

Lift Off to the Hover

With the left skid in contact, all that remains is for a smooth and positive lift-off, maintaining ground position and heading. Establish a hover at a safe height and carry out the post-take-off checks. Manoeuvre away from the slope, taking care not to turn the tail into the slope.

Airmanship

The main points of airmanship for this exercise include:

- Maintain a good lookout.
- Monitor engine and fuel instruments.
- Be aware of wind limits for out-of-wind take-offs and landings.
- Be aware of angle-of-slope limitations.

LIMITED POWER AND ADVANCED TRANSITIONS

It will not always be possible to carry out a normal transition. Hovering over loose snow, for example, may be dangerous because of reduced visibility caused by recirculation. Operating into and out of confined areas often requires a vertical descent and take-off. Under certain ambient conditions, the power margin available may be limited, and special techniques must be used for take-off and landing. No attempt will be made to limit performance by loading the helicopter with ballast, instead your instructor will restrict the manifold pressure to an appropriate figure for simulation purposes. To select the most appropriate technique, you must relate the performance required to the performance available.

Performance Required/Performance Available

You should aim to transition away heading into wind if possible. The performance required will depend on the size of obstacles on your climb-out path. If the ground ahead is level and free of obstructions, the helicopter can be transitioned into forward flight, even if there is only sufficient power for a gentle rate of climb. If there are obstacles immediately ahead, a vertical climb will be needed before transitioning into forward flight. If the obstacles are no more than about 20 ft (6 m) high, you should be able to carry out a safe transition, even if there is only sufficient power to carry out a hover IGE. If the obstacles are taller, you will only be able to transition away if you have sufficient power for a hover OGE.

The power available can be determined by either the pre-landing power check or the pre-take-off power check.

Pre-Landing Power Check

Fly straight and level at 35 kt (40 mph) and note the manifold pressure reading. Increase power to check that maximum permissible power can be obtained. The difference between the two readings is the power margin, which determines the landing capability of the helicopter. Typical power margins are given in the following table.

Manifold Pressure in Hand	Landing Capability
Less than 2 in	Run-on landing is necessary
2–4 in	Zero-speed landing is possible
5 in	2 ft hover
6 in	4 ft hover
7–8 in	Steep transition to a high hover

When flying the power check, guard against false readings obtained in gusty conditions. The check should be completed at a safe height close to the intended landing site.

Committal Height

At some point on the approach, a height will be reached below which it would be dangerous to attempt an overshoot. This height will depend not only on power available, but also on the highest obstacle on the approach and overshoot path, the nature of the landing area, and the wind and turbulence encountered. It is normal to keep 2 in of manifold pressure in hand and to maintain translational lift down to the committal height on any approach.

The Approach

The approach to a hover IGE is the normal constant-angle approach and will not be included in this exercise. The power-margin figures quoted were derived from tests carried out with a helicopter at maximum all-up weight. Therefore, it is reasonable to expect a helicopter at a lower weight to require less power to maintain straight and level flight, which would give a larger power margin. This, in turn, should lead to better performance on the approach.

Wind Effect

The power-margin figures quoted were derived in nil-wind conditions. Although an appreciable wind will reduce the power margin required for each technique, the strength of the wind at low level at the landing site will be difficult to predict exactly. For this reason, wind effect is not calculated, being treated as a bonus.

Selecting a Technique

Always aim to carry out the normal transition to hover IGE. If power is insufficient for this, you may be able to carry out a zero-speed approach to the landing site. With an even lower power margin, you will have to perform a run-on landing, provided the landing site is suitable.

The Circuit and Approach

To link the advanced transitions, a low-level, race-track-pattern circuit should be flown at 400–500 ft. Circuit speed should be 52–70 kt (60–80 mph), depending on circuit height and whether the in-flight power check is required. As you run in to the intended landing point, assess the ground speed and start your approach. Although you should continue to monitor airspeed and rate of descent, you must also scan to the side of the helicopter to make sure that your ground speed is decreasing at the required rate. The angle of approach will still be controlled with the collective lever, and heading with the pedals.

Overshoot

Anytime you are not happy with your approach, you must initiate an overshoot. During advanced transition approaches, you will have the additional problem of a limited amount of power available. Therefore, you must monitor power closely during the approach, and take any decision to overshoot as early as possible, bearing in mind that both angle of climb and rate of climb during the overshoot will be less than normal. You will need to be able to judge the point at which you have insufficient power to continue the approach. As a guide, the maximum permitted power should be used only intermittently to correct any deviations from the selected approach angle or, of course, when actually completing the landing or overshooting. If you are using maximum power more than occasionally on the approach, you must overshoot.

The Run-On Landing

With a power margin of less than 2 in of manifold pressure, a run-on landing can be carried out, provided the landing area is suitable. The speed of the run-on will increase as the power margin reduces. When established on final approach, begin a slightly shallower approach than normal and start reducing ground speed. Use the power available to maintain the approach angle. Because you intend to touch down at your aiming point, and not come to a hover above it, there will be less change in the sight picture in the latter stages of the approach than there would be in a normal approach. Fly the helicopter on to the ground, using the remaining available power to cushion the touchdown. Look well ahead and keep straight with pedals. Do not lower the collective lever fully until the helicopter has stopped. A slight lowering of the collective is acceptable if you need to reduce the length of the run-on.

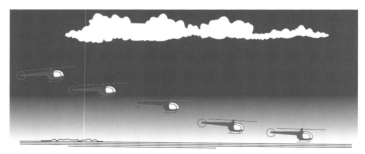

The run-on landing.

Zero-Speed Landing

This technique can be used when there is insufficient power to establish a hover, but more than is required for a run-on landing. Again, begin a slightly shallower approach than normal and start to reduce ground speed. Ground speed and rate of descent must be monitored closely, as both must have dropped to zero at the point of touch-down. In the final stages of the approach, you must maintain attitude as power is applied, so that the helicopter is level at touchdown. Make no attempt to flare off excess ground speed in the last part of the approach, as the tail could strike the ground.

Once you have landed, gently lower the collective lever to place the helicopter's weight on to the skids.

Approach to a Hover OGE

This technique can be employed whenever obstacles on the approach path prevent an angled approach to the landing point. Start a normal angle of approach, aiming for a point 10 ft above the obstacles. Reduce the ground speed during the approach, applying power as necessary to maintain the selected angle. As you approach the obstacles, use power to arrest the rate of descent and maintain ground speed at a walking pace. At this stage, you will be moving forward in a high hover taxi, maintaining height 10 ft above the obstacles. Establish a hover over your landing point, and select markers ahead and to the side. Using these markers, establish a gentle vertical descent to the normal hover height.

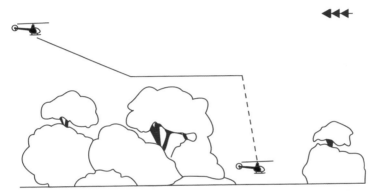

Approach to a hover OGE.

Steep Approach to Hover IGE

A steep approach should be used primarily where there are obstacles on the approach path that are too high to allow a normal approach. A steep approach will permit entry into most confined areas and sometimes is used to avoid areas of turbulence around a pinnacle. When you intercept an approach angle of about 15 degrees, reduce power to initiate the descent. Since this angle is steeper than normal, you need to lower the collective lever more than that required for a standard approach. Continue to decelerate with slight aft cyclic stick, and maintain the approach angle with power, keeping straight with pedals. Monitor the sight picture closely – it will be in a lower position in the windshield than normal. Loss of translational lift occurs higher in a steep approach, requiring an increase in power and more cyclic to achieve the proper rate of closure.

Terminate the approach at hover height above the landing point with zero ground speed. If power was applied during the latter stages of the approach, very little additional power will be required in the hover.

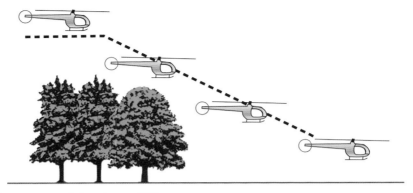

Steep approach to a hover IGE.

Pre-Take-Off Power Check

Establish a steady hover at 2 ft above the ground and heading into wind. Note the manifold pressure reading. Apply maximum authorized power. The difference between the two readings gives the power margin, which dictates the type of take-off technique available. These are given in the following table.

Manifold Pressure in Hand	Type of Take-off
Less than 1 in	Running take-off necessary
1–2 in	Cushion creep achievable
2–5 in	Towering take-off achievable
More than 5 in	Vertical-climb OGE achievable

Selecting a Take-Off Technique

If there is insufficient power for a normal transition, you should use a cushion-creep technique, provided the take-off area is suitable. If the confines of the area prevent a normal transition, you should use either a towering or vertical take-off technique, depending on the size of the obstacles and power available.

The Running Take-Off

Ensure that the take-off and climb-out paths are clear of obstacles. The best way of executing a running take-off is to raise the collective lever to apply maximum available power and gently move the cyclic stick forward to get the helicopter moving along the ground. As the speed increases, allow the helicopter to fly off. Care must be exercised as the skids break contact, since there will be a tendency for the nose to pitch down, which must be prevented with cyclic stick. The angle of climb will be very shallow, especially in light wind conditions, so you will need a long, clear take-off path.

The Cushion-Creep Take-Off

With low power margins, this technique offers an easy transition into forward flight. It utilizes the benefit of the ground cushion and allows the excess power available to be used to maintain height as the helicopter accelerates close to the ground. The climb angle will be quite shallow, so you will need a large clear area ahead of the helicopter.

From a steady hover, carry out a lookout turn, then select a reference marker. Descend to a low hover (2 ft) to obtain maximum benefit from the ground effect, then start the transition with a gentle cyclic stick movement. Prevent any sink with power and let the helicopter slowly accelerate close to the ground. At the onset of translational lift, allow the helicopter to climb slightly, but keep it accelerating. Establish the best-angle-of-climb speed – 30 kt (35 mph) – if there are obstacles ahead; once clear, however, accelerate to the best-rate-of-climb speed – 52 kt (60 mph).

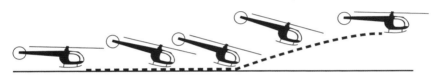

The cushion-creep take-off.

The Towering Take-Off

If the landing site has obstacles up to about 20 ft (6 m) in height and your power check indicates a power margin of 2–5 in of manifold pressure, you can transition into forward flight using the towering take-off technique.

From a steady hover, carry out a lookout turn, then select reference markers ahead and to the side. Descend to the 2 ft hover to utilize the ground effect and, when steady, increase power to the maximum available. Gentle control movements are essential, as over-controlling with cyclic stick or pedals can easily lead to a reduced power margin.

During the climb, scan between your markers to confirm that you are climbing vertically. If the helicopter is still climbing steadily as it comes level with the tops of the obstacles, you can gently transition into forward flight while maintaining a rate of climb.

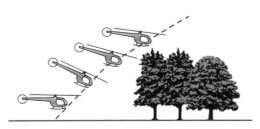

The towering take-off.

Insufficient Rate of Climb

If the rate of climb is decreasing as the helicopter becomes level with the tops of the obstacles, you must not attempt to transition into forward flight, as it would sink into the obstructions. In this case, you must descend vertically and slowly back to the hover, using the same reference markers.

Incorrect Transition Technique

Even if the helicopter has sufficient rate of climb as it becomes level with the tops of the obstacles, an incorrect transition technique could still result in it sinking toward them. If the transition is judged correctly, the helicopter will climb and accelerate. If the transition is too rapid, however, it will sink toward the obstacles while accelerating. If the transition is either too gentle or is left too late, the helicopter will also sink toward the obstacle.

The Vertical Climb

If the landing site has obstacles higher than 20 ft (6 m), you will need a power margin greater than 5 in of manifold pressure to carry out a vertical take-off. Once you have completed your lookout turn, selected your forward and side reference markers, and established a steady low hover, increase power. With a large power margin, use only enough power to give an acceptable and controllable rate of climb. When clear of the obstacles and still climbing, gently transition into forward flight. If there are further obstacles ahead, use the best-angle-of-climb speed; if not, use the best-rate-of-climb speed.

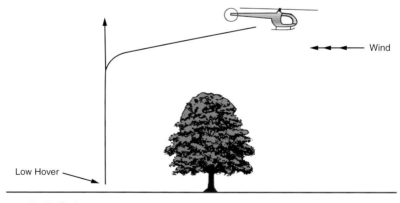

The vertical climb.

Initially, the primary objective of this exercise is for you to learn to fly the various advanced transition techniques correctly. Once you have achieved an acceptable standard, your instructor will ask you to carry out these techniques with a simulated maximum power. Toward the end of the course, you will be given a simulated maximum power, and will be expected to select and fly the appropriate technique.

CONFINED-AREA OPERATIONS

A confined area exists whenever obstructions force a steeper-than-normal approach, whenever the manoeuvring space in the ground cushion is limited, or whenever obstacles force a steeper-than-normal climb-out angle. The ability to enter, manoeuvre in and take-off from a confined area is one of the most important aspects of helicopter operations.

Reconnaissance of a Confined Area

The success of any confined-area operation depends mainly on the thoroughness with which the reconnaissance (recce) is carried out. You must assess all of the relevant factors, and to help with this, you will fly a specified pattern initially. Later on, as you gain experience, you will be encouraged to fly a shortened version, and eventually, you may be able to make a complete assessment in perhaps as little as one orbit. Some points first:

Power check You must carry out a power check to ensure that the helicopter has an OGE capability.

Wind velocity As you approach the area, make a mental note of any general wind indications. You will need this information when considering the approach direction to use.

Confined area identification You must make a positive identification of the confined area.

The complete reconnaissance follows the standard form of the five 'Ss', and can be split into two phases:

The high recce Here, you will note the major features and the general setting of the confined area. Consider the size, shape and surrounds; relating this information to the wind direction will enable you to make your initial choice of both approach direction and type of approach. Also, you should decide in which direction you would overshoot if it became necessary.

The low recce This allows a more detailed inspection to be carried out, so that you can confirm or revise your original choices. Also, you will be able to inspect the surface and slope surrounding the landing area.

The High Recce

The pattern for the high recce is an orbit flown at 52 kt (60 mph) and approximately 500 ft above the obstacles surrounding the confined area. Check the following:

Size Is the confined area large enough to enter?

Shape Which direction of approach gives sufficient length to effect a descent and landing?

215

Surrounds Consider tall obstructions around the confined area, or poor areas for over-flight in the event of an emergency.

Wind velocity The wind direction and strength will affect your choice of approach direction. While a light wind on a very different heading from your preferred flight path may be acceptable, a strong wind may force you to make an into-wind approach regardless of the difficulties posed by shape or obstructions.

At first, you will probably need to orbit several times while you assess all these factors, but it is important that you take your time. Once you have decided on the approach direction that offers the best compromise, note the heading on your compass. Using this heading:

1. Look at the two options for circuit direction. It is preferable to fly a circuit direction with the pilot's seating position on the inside to keep the confined area in view.
2. Once you have decided on the circuit direction, mentally plot a race-track circuit pattern by reference to landmarks.

When you are satisfied that you have gained sufficient information from the high recce, you will need to descend for a closer look. As you descend, watch out for wires.

The Low Recce
The low recce is carried out at 52 kt (60 mph) and 200 ft above the obstacles. Fly the race-track circuit you planned earlier, using the landmarks and your compass. The aim of the low recce is to confirm or modify the decisions you made on the high recce. Any changes you make should be only of a minor nature and probably will not require a climb up for another high recce. During the low recce, you should:

1. Confirm or reselect the following:

   • The direction and type of approach.
   • Landmarks around the circuit.
   • The best overshoot path.
   • The best climb-out path when taking-off from the confined area. Again, it may be necessary to make a compromise between the wind velocity and the obstacles. You may well climb out on a different heading from the approach.
2. Inspect the surface and slope of the ground, noting any obstructions within the confined area, and select a landing point.
3. Select markers within the confined area. A forward marker will be necessary to ensure rotor tip clearance laterally, and a lateral marker will be needed to indicate when the tail of the helicopter has cleared the obstacles on the near side of the confined area.

The low recce may take several circuits, but when you have confirmed your approach plan and studied the confined area itself, you will be ready to make your approach.

Entry to a Confined Area

Fly the circuit pattern you confirmed on your low recce, at the same height and speed. Carry out pre-landing checks when downwind, and reduce ground speed in the final-approach turn to a fast walking pace. There are three types of approach, which will be discussed separately. All have one factor in common: a strong wind blowing across the confined area may cause wind sheer and turbulence. This will erode your power margin and may require you to overshoot.

The Single-Angle Approach

Fly straight and level on the approach until the far edge of the confined area floor is visible. If an approach to this point approximates to the normal sight picture, begin a single-angle approach. During the descent, reduce the ground speed further until it is no more than a slow walking pace; aim to pass over the near side of the area with a minimum clearance of 10 ft from the obstacles. At this stage, wind sheer and turbulence can suddenly become more noticeable. Monitor power as usual, but if it becomes critical, overshoot and reassess the situation. As you enter the confined area, you must keep moving forward and not steepen the approach angle, as this could result in the tail striking the obstructions. Establish a high hover at the far side of the area, well clear of any overhanging obstructions.

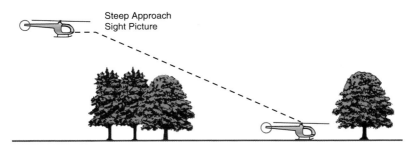

The single-angle approach.

The Double-Angle Approach

In a smaller confined area, you will not be able to see the floor at the far side when you intercept the normal approach angle. Therefore, you must make a double-angle approach, or an approach to a hover OGE followed by a vertical descent. Initiate a normal descent, aiming to pass over the near side of the area with a minimum clearance of 10 ft. Choose a background marker on the far side as an aiming point to help you maintain the normal angle of approach. During this descent, more of the confined area will become visible; when the floor at the far end can be seen clearly, change to a steeper constant-angle approach, using this as your new aiming point. The lateral marker you selected on the low recce will indicate when the tail is over a clear area. Continue forward and down to the high hover. Monitoring of speeds and power remain the same as for a single-angle approach.

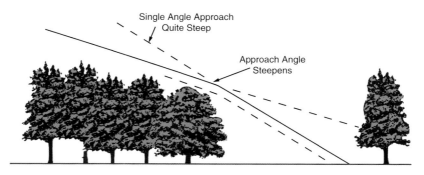

The double-angle approach.

The Approach to a Hover OGE and Vertical Descent

In a very small confined area, there may be only enough room to make a vertical descent. Fly the approach to a hover OGE, and select a background marker on the far side as an aiming point to help you maintain the normal angle of approach. Establish the hover over the centre of the confined area, as indicated by your markers. Using the markers, establish a gentle vertical descent to a high hover.

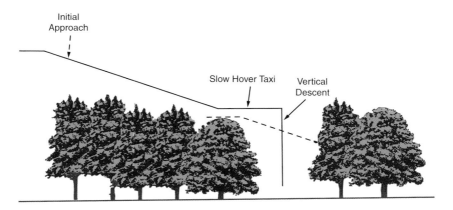

The approach to a hover OGE and vertical descent.

Overshooting
The overshoot criteria described in Advanced Transitions also apply to confined areas. If a deviation from the selected approach cannot be corrected safely, or if the power in hand becomes insufficient to continue the approach, you must overshoot, maintaining a minimum of 10 ft clearance from bstructions.

Manoeuvring in the Confined Area
Having established a high hover inside the confined area, you will need to manoeuvre to find the best landing point. When manoeuvring, always ensure that:

- The main rotor disc remains clear of overhanging branches, etc.
- The tail remains clear of all obstructions.
- The skids remain clear of any obstructions on the ground.

The most common form of manoeuvring within a confined area is a combination of sideways movement with the lookout turn. Often, this is referred to as a *turn about the tail*. This type of turn sweeps a larger area than the normal spot turn, but the tail is always in a safe position and cannot swing into obstacles. To picture this turn, it may help if you imagine the fuselage as the spoke of a bicycle wheel, with the tail as the hub. The cyclic stick is used to initiate a sideways movement. At the same time, pedal is used to turn the helicopter, while power maintains height. A slight back pressure on the cyclic stick may be required to stop the helicopter from drifting out of the turn, especially when passing through the downwind position. The rate of sideways movement is controlled by the cyclic stick, and the rate of turn by the pedals. You must manoeuvre sufficiently slowly that you can stop immediately if you notice something hazardous.

The Landing
Always land with care and use the sloping-ground techniques. Your landing direction may be dictated by the slope or obstructions within the confined area, and may not be the same as your approach direction or your planned departure path.

Take-Off and Transition from the Confined Area
To select the best departure route, you need to consider the best compromise between wind velocity, the height of the obstacles around you and the best climb-out path. Manoeuvre to the take-off point and carry out a power check facing your intended departure direction. Transition out of the confined area using the towering or vertical techniques practised earlier.

Airmanship

The main points of airmanship for this exercise are:

- Maintain a good lookout, especially when entering, manoeuvring in and departing the confined area.
- Monitor engine and fuel instruments.
- Monitor the wind velocity.
- Carry out the necessary power checks to ensure adequate power margins.
- Observe all aspects of the reconnaissance.

BASIC INSTRUMENT FLYING

Current regulations require you to receive instruction in basic instrument flying as part of your training. So far, you will have seen how flight instrument indications have been linked with actual helicopter movements, although you will have been using external references to control the machine. When flying a helicopter by reference to flight instruments, proper instrument interpretation is the basis for good control. Because of the lags and errors associated with certain instruments, any change in conditions may not be indicated immediately.

To achieve smooth positive control of the helicopter during instrument flight, you will need to develop three fundamental skills: instrument cross-check, instrument appreciation and helicopter control.

Instrument Cross-Check

Cross-checking, often called scanning, is the continuous and logical observation of instruments for attitude and performance information. In attitude instrument flying, an attitude is maintained by reference to the instruments. The actual technique may vary depending on the instruments installed, as well as your experience and proficiency level. For this exercise, you will concentrate on the six basic instruments.

Initially, you may have a tendency to cross-check rapidly, looking at instruments without knowing exactly what information you are seeking. With practice, however, scanning will start to reveal definite trends that will help you fly the helicopter more accurately. If you apply your full concentration to one instrument, you will encounter a problem known as *fixation*, which will result in poor control. You should look at each instrument only long enough to understand the information it presents, then continue to the next one. Most pilots adapt well to instrument flight after correct instruction and practice.

The six basic instruments.

Instrument Appreciation

When taken together, the flight instruments give a picture of what is happening to the helicopter. No one instrument is more important than another. During certain manoeuvres, however, the instruments that provide the most pertinent information are called the *primary* instruments. Those that back up and supplement the primary instruments are called *supporting* instruments. For example, since the attitude indicator is the only instrument that provides instant and direct attitude information, it is the primary instrument during any change in pitch and bank attitude. After the new attitude has been established, other instruments become primary, and the attitude indicator becomes a supporting instrument.

Helicopter Control

Controlling the helicopter correctly results from the accurate interpretation of the flight instruments and translation of the readings into the required control movements. Helicopter control involves adjustments to pitch, bank, power and trim to achieve a desired flight path.

Pitch attitude Controlling the helicopter about its lateral axis. After interpreting the helicopter's pitch instruments (pitch indicator, altimeter, ASI and VSI), cyclic stick adjustments are made to effect any required change.

Bank attitude Controlling the angle between the rotor disc and the natural horizon. After interpreting the bank instruments (attitude indicator, heading indicator and turn indicator), cyclic stick movements are made to attain the desire bank attitude.

Power control The application of collective pitch with corresponding throttle control, where applicable. In straight and level flight, changes of collective pitch are made to correct height deviations if the error is more than 100 ft. If the error is less than that, a slight cyclic pressure should be used to correct it. To fly a helicopter by reference to instruments, you should know the approximate power settings required for your particular machine.

Trim This refers mainly to the use of the cyclic stick centring button, if fitted, to relieve all possible cyclic loads. Trim also refers to the use of pedal adjustment to centre the ball of the turn-and-slip indicator. Pedal trim is required during all power changes.

The proper adjustment of frictions will help you to relax during instrument flight. Frictions should be set to minimize over-controlling and to prevent 'creeping', but not to such a degree that control movement is limited.

Straight and Level Flight

This consists of maintaining the desired heading, airspeed and height.

Pitch Control

The attitude indicator is used to establish the required pitch attitude. In level flight, pitch attitude varies with airspeed and CG. At a constant height and a stabilized airspeed, the pitch attitude is approximately level.

The primary pitch control instruments.

The attitude indicator This instrument gives a direct indication of the pitch attitude. In visual flight, you attain the desired pitch attitude by using the natural horizon as your reference. During instrument flight, you follow exactly the same procedure, but use the horizon bar on the instrument for reference.

You may note a small delay between control movement and a change in the instrument display. This is due to control lag in the helicopter and should not be confused with instrument lag. The instrument may show small discrepancies during manoeuvres involving acceleration, deceleration and turns.

If the miniature aircraft is not on the horizon bar after levelling off at cruising speed, adjust it as necessary. Once it has been set, leave it unchanged so that it will give an accurate pitch indication for the remainder of the flight.

When making initial corrections to pitch attitude to maintain height, the changes should be small and smooth. The initial movement of the horizon bar should not exceed one bar's width high or low. If a further change is required, an additional correction of half a bar is usually all that is required. This one-and-a-half-bar correction is normally the maximum pitch attitude correction from level flight attitude. After you have made the correction, cross-check the other pitch instruments to determine whether the change is sufficient. If more correction is needed to return to height, adjust the power.

The attitude indicator.

The altimeter This instrument gives an indirect indication of the helicopter's pitch attitude in straight and level flight. Since the height should remain constant in level flight, any deviation from it shows a need to change the pitch attitude and, if necessary, power. The rate at which the altimeter moves will help in determining pitch attitude. A very slow movement indicates a small deviation from the desired pitch attitude; a fast movement indicates a large deviation. Take any corrective action quickly with small control movements. Movement of the altimeter should always be corrected by two distinct changes in attitude: first to stop the movement, and second to return to the desired height. If the height and airspeed are more than 100 ft and 10 kt (11 mph) low, apply power at the same time. Since the altimeter provides the most pertinent information regarding pitch in level flight, it is considered a primary instrument for pitch.

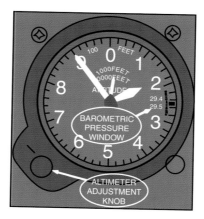

The altimeter.

The vertical speed indicator This gives an indirect indication of the pitch attitude and should be used in conjunction with the other pitch instruments. It indicates zero when in level flight. Any movement of the needle from the zero position indicates a need for an immediate pitch attitude change to return it to zero. If the correction is made promptly, usually there is little or no change in height. If you are slow to respond, the result will be shown as a gain or loss of height on the altimeter. In level flight, always use this instrument in conjunction with the altimeter. The initial movement of the needle is instantaneous, indicating the trend of the helicopter's vertical movement. A period of time is necessary for the needle to reach its maximum point of deflection after a correction has been made. This time element is commonly known as *lag*. If you use smooth control techniques and small control adjustments, lag will be minimized.

The vertical speed indicator.

The airspeed indicator This gives an indirect indication of pitch attitude. With a given power setting and pitch attitude, the airspeed remains constant. If the airspeed increases, the nose is too low and should be raised. If the airspeed decreases, the nose is too high and should be lowered. There is very little lag in the airspeed indications. Usually, a change in airspeed due to inadvertent attitude adjustment also results in a height change. For example, an increase in airspeed due to a low pitch attitude results in a loss of height.

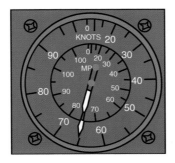

The airspeed indicator.

Bank Control

The bank attitude of a helicopter is the angular relationship between the main rotor disc and the natural horizon. To keep the helicopter on a straight heading in visual flight, you must keep the rotor disc level with the horizon. Any deviation from a laterally level attitude produces a turn. In instrument flight, the attitude indicator, heading indicator and turn indicator are used to control the helicopter's bank attitude.

The primary bank control instruments.

The attitude indicator gives you a direct indication of the helicopter's bank attitude. In instrument flying, the miniature aircraft and the horizon bar are substituted for the actual helicopter and the natural horizon. Any change in bank attitude of the helicopter is indicated instantly by the miniature aircraft. For proper interpretation of this instrument, you should imagine yourself being inside the miniature aircraft. A turn can be stopped by levelling the miniature aircraft with the horizon bar.

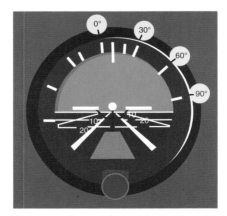

The angle of bank is shown by the pointer on top of the attitude indicator.

226

The angle of bank is indicated by the pointer on the banking scale at the top of the instrument. Pitch and bank attitudes can be determined simultaneously on this instrument.

The heading indicator In straight and level flight, the heading indicator gives an indirect indication of the helicopter's bank attitude. When a helicopter is banked, it turns, and when the rotor disc is level with the horizon, it flies straight. This means that when the heading indicator shows a constant heading, the helicopter is flying laterally level. Any deviation from the desired heading indicates a bank in the direction the helicopter is turning. A small angle of bank is indicated by a slow change of heading, while a large angle of bank will cause a rapid change of heading. If you notice a turn, apply opposite cyclic stick pressure until the heading indicator shows the correct heading again. When making a correction, do not use a bank angle greater than that required to achieve a standard rate turn (3 degrees/sec). During straight and level flight, the heading indicator is the primary bank control reference.

The heading indicator.

The turn indicator During co-ordinated flight, the needle of the turn-and-slip indicator gives an indirect indication of the helicopter's bank attitude. When the needle is displaced from the vertical position, the helicopter is turning in the direction of the needle. Cross-check the ball of the turn-and-slip indicator to ensure that the helicopter is in balanced flight – with the ball centred. You can centre the ball by 'standing on it'. For example, if the ball is displaced to the left, use left pedal to centre it; if it is out to the right, use right pedal. Always keep the ball in the turn-and-slip indicator centred by proper pedal pressure.

Inclinometer

The turn indicator.

Power Control

At any given airspeed, a specific power setting determines whether the heli-copter is in level flight, a climb or a descent. At cruise airspeed with cruise power set, the helicopter will fly level. If you increase power and maintain cruise speed, the helicopter will climb. Similarly, if you decrease power, the helicopter will descend. To maintain a constant height and airspeed in level flight, you must co-ordinate pitch attitude and power adjustments. If the height is constant and the airspeed high or low, you will have to change power to obtain the desired airspeed. If the height is low and the airspeed high, a change in pitch attitude alone may correct the situation. If both airspeed and height are low or high, changes in both power and pitch attitude will be necessary.

Primary and supporting instruments for straight and level flight.

The altimeter is the primary pitch instrument during level flight. The heading indicator remains the primary bank instrument. When changing power, the speed of the instrument scan should be increased to cover the pitch and bank instruments adequately so that any deviations can be counteracted immediately.

Procedural Climbing and Descending

As part of your introduction to instrument flying, you will be taught procedural climbing and descending. This technique requires you to maintain your cruise airspeed and adjust the power to give a 500 ft/min rate of climb or descent as necessary.

Primary and supporting instruments for climbing and descending.

Turning on Instruments

When flying by sole reference to instruments, turns should be restricted to the standard rate of 3 degrees/sec. True airspeed determines the angle of bank necessary to maintain a standard-rate turn. A rule of thumb to calculate the approximate bank angle required is to divide your airspeed by ten and add half of the result. For example, at 60 kt, approximately 9 degrees of bank is required (60/10 = 6 + 3 = 9)

To enter a turn, apply lateral cyclic stick pressure in the direction of the desired turn, using the attitude indicator to set the bank angle. When the turn indicator shows a standard-rate turn, it becomes the primary instrument for bank. Primary and supporting instruments for a level turn to the left are shown overleaf.

To recover from the turn, apply cyclic stick pressure in the opposite direction to the turn. The rate of roll out of the turn should be the same as that
used for entry. As you initiate the turn recovery, the attitude indicator
becomes primary for bank until the helicopter is level, when the heading
indicator becomes primary. Cross-check the airspeed indicator and turn-and-
slip ball closely to maintain the correct airspeed and balance.

Primary and supporting instruments for turning.

Turns on to a Pre-Determined Heading

A helicopter will continue to turn as long as the main rotor disc is tilted.
Therefore, the recovery from the turn must start before the desired heading
is reached. The amount of anticipation required will depend on the rate of
turn and your proficiency.

As a general rule, when making a standard-rate turn, use half of the bank
angle as a guide. For example, for a 12-degree bank angle, use 6 degrees as
the lead angle prior to your desired heading. As with any standard turn, the
rate of recovery should be the same as that used for the entry.

Timed Turns

A timed turn is one in which the clock and the turn indicator are used to
change heading by a definite number of degrees in a given time. For example,
in a standard turn, a helicopter turns through 45 degrees in 15 sec, 90 degrees
in 30 sec, and 180 degrees in a minute. You should employ the same scan and
control techniques required for other turns, but use the clock for the heading
indicator. Begin the roll-in as the clock's second hand passes a cardinal point.
Hold the turn at the standard rate indication and start the roll-out when the
calculated number of seconds has elapsed. If the roll-in and roll-out rates are
the same, the time taken during entry and recovery need not be considered in
the time calculations.

Climbing and Descending Turns
For climbing and descending turns, the techniques outlined earlier should be combined. For training, start the climb or descent first, then roll into the turn. The level-off from a climbing or descending turn is the same as the level-off from a straight climb or descent. To recover to straight and level flight, you may stop the turn and then level off; level off and then stop the turn; or level off and stop the turn simultaneously. During climbing and descending turns, keep the turn indicator centred with the pedals.

Recovery from Unusual Attitudes

It cannot be overemphasized that you must trust your instrument indications; disregard any physiological sensations, as they could mislead you. Failing to believe the instruments can aggravate these sensations, leading to disorientation and the helicopter entering an unusual attitude.

Your instructor will demonstrate these problems by manoeuvring the helicopter while you close your eyes. When you are given control, the aim is to make a quick interpretation of the instruments and recover smoothly to straight and level flight with the minimum loss of height.

To recover from an unusual attitude, correct the bank and pitch first, then adjust power as necessary. Since the displacement of the controls used in the recovery may be greater than for normal flight, care must be taken to prevent over-controlling.

Emergencies

Any emergencies encountered during instrument flight should be handled in a similar manner to those met under visual conditions. An autorotation and descent through cloud will be extremely hazardous, however, as you will be descending through the safety height into unknown terrain.

Entry into autorotation is exactly the same as for visual flight. Lower the collective fully to maintain a safe rotor rpm, and apply right pedal to control balance. Select the minimum rate of descent speed with the cyclic stick and trim. Check the pitch attitude indicator to ensure that the helicopter is level. Carry out emergency drills as appropriate. If you are still in cloud as you approach the safety height, adjust airspeed as for a constant-attitude autorotation. On breaking cloud (normally simulated at 800 ft), transfer from instruments to visual flight.

Instrument Take-Off

This manoeuvre is only performed as part of your introduction to instrument training. A general description of the procedure has been provided; it should be modified to suit to your particular helicopter.

Establish a steady hover facing into wind and carry out the pre-take-off checks. Adjust the miniature aircraft in the attitude indicator. Then the helicopter should be climbed vertically at full power until a positive climb is indicated, when it should be eased gently into forward flight – ensure a rate of climb is maintained. As climb airspeed is reached, reduce power to climb settings and transition to a normal, co-ordinated straight climb. Throughout the instrument take-off, scanning and interpretation must be rapid and accurate. Control of the helicopter must be positive and smooth.

Controlled Descent Through Cloud (QGH)

In essence, this is a fairly simple procedure to bring the helicopter safely down through cloud to enable you to complete your approach and landing visually.

You will home overhead the airfield at a height and heading instructed by ATC. Next, you will be turned on to an outbound heading. This turn should be carried out at a standard rate of 180 degrees/min. The outbound leg will be timed by ATC, and then you will be instructed to turn on to an inbound heading. When steady on the inbound heading, you will be cleared to descend to your approach minima. The descent should be carried out at 500 ft/min. If you are still in cloud when you reach your approach minima, you must abort the descent and carry out a missed approach procedure.

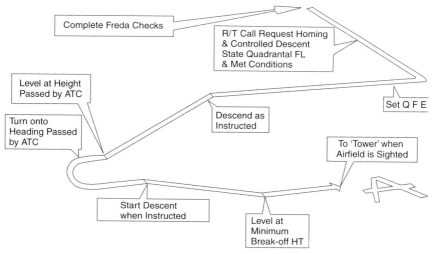

Controlled descent through cloud.

Missed Approach Procedure

This procedure combines the techniques of levelling off from a descent and those used for climbing. Apply climb power, maintain a level attitude and control balance, and settle in the climb. Obey all further instructions given by ATC.

Radar Approaches

The two procedures most commonly used are the surveillance radar approach (SRA), and the precision approach radar (GCA).

After your radio request for the approach, you will receive instructions and be guided into a radar approach procedure. ATC will position you at a safe height and distance from the instrument runway, from where you can be monitored safely throughout the descent. During both types of approach, a 3-degree angle of approach will be flown, with a descent rate of 400–500 ft/min. Procedural rates of turn are always employed.

You must initiate a missed approach procedure if you reach your approach minima without gaining visual references, or if radio contact is lost.

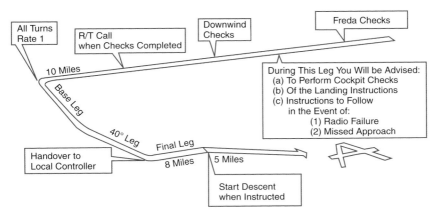

Radar approach.

Airmanship

The most common problems encountered when you first begin your instrument training are:

- Failing to fly attitudes.
- Over-controlling, especially in the pitching plane, caused by chasing the airspeed.
- Not maintaining a good selective scan.

NIGHT FLYING

You will find night flying a most enjoyable experience. In many respects, flying at night is easier and more pleasant than operating in daytime, because the air is generally cooler and smoother, giving a more comfortable flight. The handling of the helicopter is the same, and quite straightforward for a pilot who has received instrument training.

Lights

All aircraft operating between sunset and sunrise are required to have operable navigation lights. The lights displayed on an aircraft not only indicate its presence, but also can be used to determine its position relative to you.

All helicopters have a landing light to illuminate the ground when necessary. This light is used during night take-offs and landings. Care must be taken to avoid shining this light in the direction of other aircraft.

Anti-collision lights are fitted to most aircraft and consist of either a rotating beacon or high-energy flashing lights.

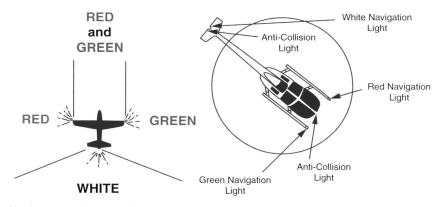

Navigation and anti-collision lights.

Night Vision

The ability to see at night can be improved if you understand and employ certain techniques. It takes the rods in the eye about 30 min to adjust to night conditions, but if you expose your eyes to a bright light, even briefly, your night vision will be destroyed temporarily. Red light has been found to be the least detrimental to night vision. However, its use can result in the disturbance of normal colour relationships.

Off-Centre Vision

Central vision is normally used to see objects during the daytime, but it is ineffective at night. For this reason, you should not look directly at an object

234

at night. Objects can be seen more clearly if your line of sight is concentrated slightly above, below or to the side of an object.

Pre-Flight Procedures

At night, you will be using some items of helicopter equipment that normally are not required during the day. It is essential, therefore, that you are fully aware of the switch positions to select this equipment and of the various methods of operation. The equipment and switches include:

- Instrument lighting, switch and dimmer.
- Navigation light, anti-collision lights and switches.
- Wander lamp, filter and switch.
- Night flares, switches and firing buttons.
- Landing lamp and on/off switch.

External Checks

Remember that the helicopter will be fitted with pyrotechnic flares for night flying. Carry out the external checks with the aid of a torch, but when you arrive at the flares, stop, then go back around the helicopter until you get to the other side of the flares, Then continue with the external checks. **Always treat the flares as being live**.

Light Signals

The following light signals are used to communicate your intentions to the ground crew:

1. Ready to start engine – navigation lights off/on.
2. Ready to engage rotor – anti-collision light on.
3. Call in ground crew to the helicopter – flash your torch.
4. Dismiss ground crew – landing lamp on/off.

Start-Up and Rotor Engagement

Before getting strapped in, remove the flare master pins and put them away safely. Carry out the normal internal and pre-start-up checks. Using the light signals described, start the engine and engage the rotor.

Leaving Dispersal

When all the checks have been completed and clearance has been obtained from ATC, switch on the landing lamp and establish a steady hover. A landing light usually casts a narrow beam that is concentrated ahead of the helicopter, so illumination to the side is minimal. Some helicopters have a hover light, which will illuminate a large area under the machine. Do not stare into the pool of light, but look well ahead and use the general all-round illumination. Judgement of distances will be quite difficult at first, so you should hover taxi slightly higher and slower than normal. On the way out to the take-off area, check that all the instruments are functioning normally. When you reach the take-off area, land with the flares pointing in a safe direction and select the flares master switch to 'ON'. **The flares are now armed**.

The Circuit and Landing

All R/T calls for take-off should be made from the hover; there is no need for a lookout turn. When cleared for take-off, carry out a towering take-off. At about 300 ft, if it is safe to do so, turn off the landing lamp. Continue to climb straight ahead and level out at 1,000 ft.

Drift appreciation diminishes at night, so the selection of heading and track references on all legs assumes a greater importance.

Carry out the normal downwind checks and, when abeam the landing point, make the 'Downwind' R/T call to signify your wish to make an approach and landing.

When you are established on final approach, make the R/T call, 'Final'. If the landing point is available, ATC will clear you to land. If the landing point is occupied, you will be cleared to 'Continue'.

The approach technique will depend on the type of landing aid being used. One rather basic, but effective, landing aid is the proportional flarepath.

Three lights are placed 40 ft (12 m) apart. In line with the centre light, a fourth light is positioned 160 ft (48 m) downwind to produce a 'T' shape. A fifth light (line-up) is placed a further 330 ft (100 m) downwind from that.

Using the line-up marker to position the helicopter on the final approach path to the 'T', you should aim to maintain a constant 'T' aspect throughout the descent. At about 300 ft, switch on the landing light and continue the approach, maintaining the 'T' picture. As you arrive at the hover, gently move over to one side to a landing point.

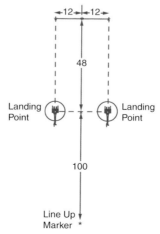

The proportional flarepath.

Going Around (Overshooting)
If for any reason, you are not able to maintain a safe approach or have not been given clearance to land by 200 ft, a go-around must be initiated. As you begin the climb, turn 45 degrees toward the circuit and call, 'Going around.' When you reach a point abeam the landing 'T', turn back on to circuit heading and carry out another circuit. If the go-around is initiated below 200 ft, do not turn, unless you need to avoid overflying other helicopters.

Entering Cloud Inadvertently
If you enter cloud inadvertently, you must go on instruments immediately and inform ATC. You may find the glare from the anti-collision beacons disorientating, in which case, switch them off until you are clear of cloud again.

Practice Forced Landing
On the downwind leg, carry out the HASEL checks and call, 'Downwind for autorotation.' Maintain height and speed on the base leg and, after turning on to final approach, call 'Final for autorotation.' Enter autorotation as normal and simulate firing the flares in quick succession. Switch on the landing light and reduce speed to achieve a constant-attitude EOL. Re-engage the rotor and initiate a go-around by 200 ft, informing ATC.

Returning to the Parking Area
On your last approach, inform ATC that your detail is complete and land with the flares pointing in a safe direction. Turn the flare master switch to 'OFF'. Lift off to the hover and call, 'Safe', for taxi back to dispersal.

Emergencies
Emergencies at night will be no different to those experienced during the day. However, lighting and radio failures will cause particular problems.

Cabin light failure At the time of failure, either use your torch or adjust the wander lamp to illuminate the instrument panel. Check that the instrument light switch is set to 'ON' and that the dimmer is turned up. If the failure is confirmed, turn the switch off.

Navigation light/beacon failure Normally, you will be informed of these failures by other aircraft or ATC. Check the switches; if the failure is confirmed, set them to 'OFF'. Complete the circuit and return to the parking area. Remember that you can see other helicopters, but they cannot see you.

Landing lamp failure Inform ATC, switch the landing light off, continue with a careful approach, land and wait for further instructions.

Total electrics failure Carry out the necessary drills and continue the circuit using your torch. Remember that your radios will also have failed. Land at the touch-down point, shut down and try to attract the attention of ATC with your torch. Use your torch to warn other helicopters of your presence. If the failure occurs away from the circuit, rejoin carefully, noting the position of other helicopters, and land at the touch-down point.

Radio failure After confirming the failure, conform to the normal circuit pattern, but extend the downwind leg slightly. From about 500 ft on final approach, switch the landing light on and off at five-second intervals, then leave it on from 200 ft and continue as normal. In the hover, turn toward ATC and flash the landing light until you are answered with a *green* light. This clears you back to the parking area.

Navigation at Night

Pre-flight planning for a night flight is the same as for daytime navigation. When studying the map, consider the features that you think will be prominent at night, e.g. towns, motorways, etc. Obstruction lights and airfield beacons can be of use, as can water features in moonlit conditions. Mark these features on your map so that they will show up even under the red wander lamp – do *not* use red chinagraph.

The flight should be conducted in a similar manner to a daytime navigation exercise. Divide your attention between events outside the helicopter and accurate flying/map reading in the cabin.

Airmanship

The main points of airmanship for this exercise are:

- Maintain a good lookout for obstructions when taxiing, and other aircraft at all times.
- Monitor engine and fuel instruments, especially when away from the circuit.
- Monitor wind velocity – significant wind variation can occur between the surface and 1,000 ft at night. Be aware of drift and wind sheer.
- Comply with all R/T procedures; listen out for other R/T calls in the circuit.
- Make sure you know the light signals used when starting up at night.
- Make sure you know the procedures for night emergencies.

INDEX